Simon Says GOLD

Simon Whitfield's Pursuit of Athletic Excellence

SIMON WHITFIELD
WITH CLEVE DHEENSAW

ORCA BOOK PUBLISHERS

D1009985

Library and Archives Canada Cataloguing in Publication

Whitfield, Simon, 1975-

Simon says gold : Simon Whitfield's pursuit of athletic excellence / written by Simon Whitfield with Cleve Dheensaw.

ISBN 978-1-55469-141-8

1. Whitfield, Simon, 1975- --Juvenile literature. 2. Athletes--Canada--Biography-- Juvenile literature. 3. Triathlon--Juvenile literature. 4. Olympics--Participation, Canadian--Juvenile literature. I. Dheensaw, Cleve, 1956- II. Title.

GV1061.15.W46A3 2009   j796.42'57092   C2009-903352-6

First published in the United States, 2009

Library of Congress Control Number: 2009929366

Summary: Autobiography of Simon Whitfield, triathlon's first Olympic gold medallist.

Orca Book Publishers gratefully acknowledges the support for its publishing programs provided by the following agencies: the Government of Canada through the Book Publishing Industry Development Program and the Canada Council for the Arts, and the Province of British Columbia through the BC Arts Council and the Book Publishing Tax Credit.

Design by Teresa Bubela
Front cover image courtesy of The Canadian Press/Adam Butler
Back cover images courtesy of the Whitfield family (far left and centre);
The Canadian Press/Adam Butler (2nd from left) and Joel Filliol (far right)
See page 116 for interior photo credits

Orca Book Publishers
PO Box 5626, Stn. B
Victoria, BC Canada
V8R 6S4

Orca Book Publishers
PO Box 468
Custer, WA USA
98240-0468

www.orcabook.com
Printed and bound in Canada.

12 11 10 09 • 4 3 2 1

Family and friends,
You mean everything to me.
Absolutely everything.
—S.W.

To my family,
and to Simon and all the athletes from our Island,
who have provided me such Olympian copy over the years.
—C.D.

CONTENTS

Adam van Koeverden and I have become great friends; we share the bond of relentless drive and commitment. He's one of the most competitive athletes I've ever met and has been rewarded with three Olympic medals, including gold at Athens. Here with the Gold Medal Crew: Kyle Shewfelt, Adam, me and Alexandre Despatie (L–R).

Adam van Koeverden
Olympic Gold Medallist

I sat alone at 4:00 AM, draped in my Canadian flag, watching the Sydney 2000 Summer Olympics Opening Ceremonies, feeling as though I wasn't invited to my best friend's birthday party. I hadn't qualified for the Olympic Games, and the true sadness didn't set in until I saw my fellow athletes march in.

In hindsight, it was a good thing I stayed home. I was too young, too slow, and I needed the kick in the pants to take my motivation to the next level. It was right then, as I wiped a tear from my cheek with the flag, that I decided that getting to the Athens 2004 Summer Olympics wasn't merely my objective, or an aspiration, it was going to be my obsession. I was going to make it my reality.

Two days later I asked myself the most important question I've ever contemplated. As I watched this skinny guy from Canada blast through his competition and rip that finish line down, stomping it into the ground, all I could think was, If this guy can do it, why can't I? That day, Simon Whitfield ignited a nation. He introduced Canada and the world to a sport that few were previously familiar with and made it one that all Canadians could feel proud about. We were, after all, a newly founded world power in the sport of triathlon! Simon's performance gave me the guts and audacity to believe that I could be the best as well. He reminded me that great performances in endurance sports are all about effort, and that world records are there to be broken.

Over the next few years I got a little bit better every season, slowly closing in on my ultimate goal of one day going to the Olympic Games and trying to beat everyone in the whole world in a kayak race. In the summer of 2002, I was on my way to a World Cup somewhere in Europe, walking through the Toronto airport, when I saw someone familiar, although we had never met. I thought I'd better introduce myself to Simon Whitfield, mostly because it felt a little awkward knowing who he was without him knowing that I knew. Plus I was pretty stoked to meet a guy who had been so inspirational for me and all the guys I trained alongside.

"We've never met before, but I'm an athlete too, and I want to thank you for helping me get closer to what I want to accomplish," I said. After a brief exchange, we went our separate ways. Simon wished me good luck, and off we went to race.

Two years later, during the Opening Ceremonies of the Athens 2004 Olympic Games, I once again sat, sad, in a basement. This time in France, wondering why I was missing out on that incredible celebration of sport. After all, I had qualified this time; I had a spot on the team. I felt it was unfair that our team decided to miss the Opening Ceremonies and go into Greece at the very last minute, just a few days before our competition. (In hindsight, however, this proved to be an excellent decision.) I expressed my discontent to my coach Scott Oldershaw, to which he jokingly replied, "Whatever. Just carry the flag at the Closing Ceremonies; then you won't care about missing the Opening." We both laughed, and the image of Simon carrying the Canadian flag into the Closing in Sydney flashed through my mind.

Two weeks later, I crossed the finish line first in front of the whole world in a kayak race and became an Olympic champion. I too was selected to carry our flag at the Closing Ceremonies. It was the proudest moment of my life. I had truly believed in myself, and in Scott's wisdom and advice. That strong belief, really hard work and so much inspiration helped to get me to the finish line first.

I call it *reciprocal inspiration*, when one person's accomplishments live on and encourage more people to believe in themselves and accomplish their own goals. As I see it, there are three incredible features of this phenomenon: it doesn't expire, it can be shared among an unlimited number of people and it has the capacity to cross genres and disciplines. A triathlete can inspire a kayaker, a musician, an artist and a young child, and they can each go on to inspire others and continue the cycle.

In Beijing at the 2008 Summer Olympics, I watched Simon get inspired by the fantastic gold-medal performance of the Canadian men's rowing eights. After watching the rowers win, both triumphant and vindicated, Simon put forth one of the best races of his career, and I watched, screaming my brains out. That afternoon, only a few hours later, I broke the world record in the K-1 500-metre race in Beijing. I don't think it was a coincidence that I had one of my greatest races ever after watching my friend have one of his. And I know it was no coincidence that Simon had a reminder of the men's eight rowing team written on his handlebars.

Therein lies one of the most significant and valuable aspects of sport: its ability to uplift, inspire and motivate. Every Olympian was once an inspired child, and I don't think the power of that inspiration, coupled with a goal, can ever be overstated. Simon's performance in Sydney encouraged me to reconsider the limitations I had put on myself, and drove me to believe that I was capable of something that was, at the time, very, very out of reach. And all with one simple question: Why not me? Dreams are important. If there is anything I try to encourage kids to do, it's to first imagine themselves somewhere far away—way up high, someplace that seems unattainable—then I tell them that the next step is to begin planning how they will get there. Thanks for helping me do that, Simon.

ADAM VAN KOEVERDEN
MAY 2009

My name in lights. Simon Whitfield, GOLD MEDALLIST. Wow! The medal ceremony, and the tears were about to flow.

CHAPTER 1

Sydney 2000

The morning of September 17, 2000, dawned sunny and bright in Sydney, Australia. I awoke a largely unknown and unheralded Olympic triathlete. The day would not end that way. Yet I had no way of knowing that as I slipped out of bed in my dorm in the Athletes Village of the 2000 Summer Olympics. Surprisingly, I had slept extremely well the night before my first Olympic race. Perhaps that goes with being so far off the form charts—the ones that listed the favourites—as the sport of triathlon was making its long-awaited debut in the Olympic Games. Perhaps my greatest claim to fame at this point was the bronze medal I had won the year before in the 1999 Pan American Games. Bronze medals won in regional games are not about to get any world-class opponent shaking in his sneakers or the media clamouring for interviews. Nobody was talking about me. In many ways, that was good. There was no pressure and I felt loose.

There had been some hiccups with our Canadian team's pre-Games period in Sydney, but we just rolled with it. It was all part of the certain freshness in the air. Our sport was young and just learning how to operate the ropes on the biggest stage that sport provides.

Sharon "Captain" Donnelly and me, playing it up for the camera. Our whole team was very relaxed before the races. I was just a kid in Sydney, and that attitude put me on the start line in a perfect state of mind.

And so were we as athletes. The Canadian squad arrived from ten days of training at Bond University on the Gold Coast. We were the least-stressed group of Olympic athletes you can imagine. There was a calm that hung over us that was hard to explain. Little was expected of me, and although I harboured a deep and burning ambition to succeed, my coach Lance Watson and I revelled in the looseness of this moment. One particular moment that stands out in the lead-up was that I had put in an absolutely crushing training run on the Gold Coast. I felt spring-loaded. Even though I wasn't much fancied on the form charts, I knew I was ready to give it a good shot in Sydney. Sometimes an athlete just feels it. This was one of those moments. When I finished that workout on the Gold Coast, Lance almost didn't know what to say. As an athlete often does, especially a younger athlete, I looked for confirmation from my coach that I had indeed run as fast as I felt I had. Lance just smiled, clapped his hands together and said, "You are absolutely ready, Simon. That was just jaw-dropping impressive." Okay, then, I guess I was ready.

Because the men's Olympic triathlon race was scheduled two days after the Opening Ceremonies, we did not march in with the rest of the athletes. Little did I know then that I would be carrying in the Canadian flag during the Closing Ceremonies sixteen days later.

The Canadian men's field-hockey team had a game scheduled the next day against Pakistan, so they did not march in the Opening Ceremonies either. We sat as a group, watching the ceremonies on television. From our Canadian dorm we could actually see the mighty Stadium Australia at Homebush Bay and hear the thunderous roar of the crowd and see the sparkle of the fireworks as the ceremonies unfolded. At just the moment the Canadian team entered the stadium, Ravi Kahlon of the field-hockey team suddenly grabbed a stick and tied a Canadian flag to it. Inspired, we got behind our impromptu flag-bearer and marched through the streets of the Athletes Village, singing "O Canada" in our very own private Opening Ceremonies. It was a moment I will never forget.

The women's race was the next day, and Bridget McMahon of Switzerland became the first women's Olympic gold medallist in triathlon history. We all revelled in the moment. Only a few years earlier, this sport I loved was often thought to be for the lunatic fringe and practiced only by a bunch of crazies in bright Speedos. Now look at it. We were in the Olympics and we had our first gold medallist in Bridget. If for a fleeting moment I even dared to think I would become her counterpart the next day, as the first men's Olympic champion in our sport, I can't remember it. I felt relaxed and under no pressure, outside of the quiet, building confidence that I was capable of something special. Feeling it and doing it, however, are two different things.

Bridget's victory was tempered for me by the disaster that struck my Canadian teammates in the women's Olympic race. Sharon Donnelly had crashed, and I gave her a hug when she returned to the Village. It was done and over. I thought to myself I could best help Sharon and the rest of our women's team by doing well the next day.

That day came soon enough. The whole morning before the Olympic race flowed nicely for me. What surprised me most was not how loose I felt but how uptight and nervous many of my competitors, especially the favourites, seemed to be. The Olympics will do that to you. This is not just another race. Handling the immense pressure of the Games is the greatest task for any Olympian. I had it bottled and under control. The others didn't. Everybody else seemed so serious and had stern looks on their faces.

The first carriage, an old shockingly yellow school bus, arrived at the Village to whisk the competitors to the venue, and the nervous bulk of the racers crowded aboard. It was cramped, and it buzzed, ready to burst not with excitement but with tension. So I held back with a couple of other racers and noticed a luxurious cruiser bus pulling in behind. We asked if it too was for triathlete transport and the volunteers said yes. We climbed aboard and had a much more restful and relaxing ride than the athletes crowded on the old school bus in front of us. That was when I learned one of my greatest Olympic lessons: Take it easy. Relax. Breathe.

The bus transported us to the dock, where we would catch the ferry that would take us to the start line across the harbour. Aussie spring was officially still a few days away and the morning, although bright, was cool. While the bulk of my competitors and their coaches and managers shivered on the dock, awaiting the ferry, Stephan Vuckovic of Germany and I noticed two chairs in a warm shelter building. We tried the door. It was open, so we entered and sat and waited for the ferry, again in relative comfort. The level of tension was high and rising by the minute on the crowded dock, but there were Vuko and I with our feet casually up on a table looking out through the windows and taking it all in. Yes, this was the same bald-headed German with whom I would share the stage only a few hours later in a mad dash to the finish line.

Here he was just staring at void ticket stubs, while I, for some strange reason, couldn't get "Waltzing Matilda" out of my head.

Barrie Shepley, the Canadian team triathlon manager and overall coach, had a way of keeping it light to take your mind off the race. I will never forget his banter that morning as he tried to keep us calm. "What gas mileage do you get in your car at home, Simon?" "Look at that building, Simon. Isn't that an interesting architectural design?" I just smiled. I felt so relaxed and at peace as it was. Barrie's chatter simply added to the lightness of the moment. "What's the colour of the front door on your house at home, Simon?" he asked. I answered, "Barrie, I'm a Canadian amateur athlete. Shouldn't you be asking 'What colour is your tent?'" We laughed.

The one small problem we faced was that we were limited to one coaching accreditation for the triathlon team, and as a result, my personal coach, Lance Watson,

 TRIATHLON 101

Everybody knows triathlon involves swimming, biking and running in that order. Here are the basics of my sport:

ORIGINS: *I love reading about triathlon history. According to the great American triathlon legend, historian and author Scott Tinley, the first recorded mention of a triathlon race was in France in 1920, and the order of sports was running first, followed by cycling and ending with swimming.*

MODERN ORIGINS: *The first modern triathlon was held at Mission Bay near San Diego in 1974. As a modern sport, we are not that old—a baby really in world timeline sporting terms.*

had to watch the proceedings from behind a fence. Still, we'd gone through the race plan—strong start in the swim, positioning on the bike, being prepared to hurt on the run. Whether Lance was behind a fence or not, we both knew the preparation was finished.

Yet I was still only ranked twenty-sixth in the world. As the fifty Olympic finalists gathered at the start line, I looked across and there was the great five-time world champion Simon Lessing of Britain, the first true legend of what became known as Olympic-distance triathlon, and the reigning world champion Olivier Marceau of France. I was in position three and directly next to me in the first two of the fifty starting slots were European champion Andrew Johns of Britain and world top-ranked Hamish Carter of New Zealand. But instead of being intimidated, I felt strong and secure. And just a little playful.

I turned to Hamish at the start line and said, "I hope the sharks don't bite us when we jump into this harbour."

Instead of laughing, Hamish seemed nervous and certainly confused by my looseness and jocularity at this very serious Olympian moment. He was under tremendous pressure and expectation. The New Zealand media had already counted his medal.

"What?" he said, rather incredulously, as he stared across at me. He didn't say anything else but his face read *Get away from me.*

Standing on the start line can be so nerve-racking. That's me, third from the left, likely still laughing at my joke about the sharks. As relaxed as I was, I was ready to perform and had a clear vision of the race in my mind's eye.

It wasn't until we were into the bike portion of the race that I realized I was really ready to have a special day. Miles Stewart from Australia, Ben Bright from New Zealand and I came out of the water a little bit back of the leaders but worked together to rein in the lead pack. I remember thinking to myself, This is going to be a special, special day.

He must have been thinking the loonies from Canada aren't just the ones on the one-dollar coin.

Then *BANG!* And we were off.

My first Olympic race, and the first in Summer Games history, had begun. The next 1,500 metres of swimming, forty kilometres of bike riding and ten kilometres of running would decide the inaugural men's Olympic champion. I dove into Sydney Harbour and churned furiously. I wasn't a strong swimmer at the time, so I was satisfied when I emerged from the water in twenty-seventh position. Nobody, least of all me, was yet predicating gold, however.

I got on the bike without a hitch after the transition and immediately felt I was riding well. Ben Bright of New Zealand, Miles Stewart of Australia and I comprised the front of a small second chase pack about forty-five seconds down on the lead group. We worked together and rolled into the back of the lead pack. I thought to myself, Wow, I'm in the Olympics and I'm in the lead pack!

Simon Lessing looked across at me and seemed ambivalent. He was five-time world champion and I a mere up-and-comer.

Back home at one of my training venues in Victoria, British Columbia, I had named one of the running trails at Thetis Lake *Lessing Lane* in honour of him. And now here I was, shoulder-to-shoulder with the legend and several others, jostling in the lead pack on the bike.

The Aussies are great sports fans, and the crowd noise was beginning to swell along the route. The pace was now pulsating and so was the mounting atmosphere. Sydney was in my ears. I was pumped and went right by Lessing. My next thought was one of amazement: Wow, I'm in the lead of the cycling pack at the Olympic Games! I had never before been in the lead of the cycling pack at a major championship.

My sense of euphoria didn't last long, however, as I had to keep focused on the task at hand. Then suddenly, near disaster! I looked up and saw a group of crashed cyclists in a heap immediately ahead of me. I had no time to avoid them and skidded right into the mess. Fortunately I managed to keep my feet beneath me and was the only one from the crash to make it back on the bike in quick fashion. Had my reaction been a split second slower, I would have gone head over heels, and the outcome of this day would have been much different.

The difference between Olympic glory and heartbreak is often balanced on such a fine line, and I've thought about that a lot in the ensuing years. But in the pulsing emotion of an Olympic race, you have little time for such reflection. I simply got back on my bike and began instinctively pedaling as if my very being depended on it. In many ways, it did. When I caught the lead pack for the second time in the same race, the quiet confidence that was brewing inside me was simply reinforced.

I was seventeenth off the bike. There was a large jumble in the transition area, and heading out I was near the back end of the lead group. Running has always been the strongest of the three disciplines in triathlon for me. It was my entry into the sport. It was what I did in high school athletics and had always been my strength in my chosen sport.

Feeling spry and with reservoirs of energy remaining, I began running through the lead pack until I made it to the front. I was now

Stephen Vuckovic was such a strong man and used this strength to push the downhills and gain advantage. He made his play for victory here at the turn around at the top of Macquarie Street.

running with the likes of Simon Lessing, Miles Stewart, Peter Robertson of Australia and Ivan Rana of Spain. These were all competitors I had looked up to and admired. Though I didn't know it at the time, the defending world champion, Olivier Marceau of France, who was reported to have spent the previous three months training out of a monastery in the French Alps, had made a breakaway with two other competitors late into the bike and was now alone out front and leading the Olympic triathlon by thirty seconds. This, however, was not to be his day. This was to be the day of the unknown Canadian. My body seemed super-charged, with all muscles straining and my mind clear. Focused and determined, I just seemed to flow forward. I noticed that most of the others in the lead pack weren't nearly as fresh, and soon they started fading as this little-known Canadian surged.

Seven kilometres, eight kilometres, nine kilometres. The metres melted away until I could hear a crescendo of noise up ahead and around the bend where the finish line awaited. Now only Stephan Vuckovic of Germany—my "waiting" partner from the morning at the ferry dock—and I remained. We were shoulder to shoulder. We had relentlessly pulled away from the rest of the pack, although Jan Rehula of the Czech Republic and Dmitriy Gaag of Kazakhstan had us within sighting distance, and the Kazak was known to be a tremendous closer. A key moment came earlier when Vuckovic and I had passed on either side of the French "monk"—defending world champion Marceau—at eight kilometres. It was then I turned to Vuckovic and said, "Holy crap. We're leading the Olympic Games!"

Now that breath and energy was at a premium, I probably should not have wasted precious oxygen by making that remark. Every breath and every metre counted at this moment. The descent from Hyde Park to the finish line was mostly downhill. Vuckovic had pulled a few metres ahead but I noticed something. He was running down the middle of the road while I consciously took the curb. Though the middle of the road appeared to be the best line, it was actually the inside curb which provided the best route, something my coach Lance had noted on our pre-race run-through. I remembered that and it stuck with me as I hugged tight to the curb, oblivious to the screaming spectators only inches away. Vuko had some reprieve from the noise, but I had the better line. It suddenly came to me that I could catch Vuckovic, and I started sprinting for all I was worth. I thought to myself, Screw it, here we go. Stephan has made his move and it hasn't worked. He has played his cards and doesn't have any others to play. He's got nothing left, and I do.

Lance had said to me before the race, "When you sprint, do it like a kid chasing a ball and give it everything you have." All those games in youth soccer had served a purpose—in the Olympic triathlon race, of all things! Who could have known? Lance was basically saying, Let go of the fear of the consequences. Relax and sprint like you stole something!

I caught Vuckovic, and not a moment too soon. There were only a hundred metres remaining. I flew past him, and he could not respond to my push. I was running away from him. Running toward what felt like my destiny. Running toward Olympic glory and gold. Running toward a finish-line banner that every Olympian dreams of crossing first.

While jogging back home in Victoria, along the trails at Thetis Lake, I had played out this moment in my mind so many times, and I dared to believe it could come true. It was also born out of my creative pursuits and endless games as a kid—driven by a passion to do something extraordinary and born from an inherent belief that "What you believe, you will achieve."

My great friend and training partner Jasper Blake, an Ironman-distance champion, used to joke while running at Thetis Lake about what I would do at the moment of Olympic greatness if ever it came. I used to tell Jasper if I ever approached the Olympic finish line in first place, "I'm going to yell 'How's that?'"

And that's exactly what I did that morning in the shadow of the Sydney Opera House. As the finish line drew closer with every passing step, I looked up and screamed, "How's that?"

"How's that?" I had a clear vision of what I wanted to do in Sydney, and I'd played that finish-line scene over and over in my mind for years.

How's that, world? "Olympic Champion" sure has a nice ring. Strike up the band. Play the anthem! I had pictured this moment in my head so many times, of breasting the tape and then throwing it to the ground. Crossing the line and looking up at the surging crowd of 25,000 at the finish, the magic of it all suddenly hit me. It is one thing to dream about it and another to actually cross the line first.

My gosh, this did actually happen, didn't it? was my immediate thought. Then there seemed a million other excited thoughts rushing through my head. So many that I could barely process them all. It felt as if my brain would explode. A movie of my life played out right before my eyes. I thought about accomplishing this feat in the city where my father was from and where I had attended high school. I thought about the amazing coincidence of crossing the finish line as Olympic champion just a few metres from where I attended my high school graduation ceremonies on the steps of the Opera House. I thought about my ninety-six-year-old grandmother—"Nana"—who lived with us when I was younger and often told my sister and me to dream big. She was just across Sydney Harbour from where I was, watching this race on TV in her nursing home because physically she could not be at the finish line. She hadn't run a step in years, but that day I heard she did three laps of the cribbage table and a cartwheel on the shuffleboard track.

Canadian coach Barrie Shepley was crying as he came to embrace me. Behind the fence enclosure, my coach Lance Watson was jumping up and down and going ballistic. We all were. As I made my way to doping control, I was grabbed by a large group of my old Aussie high-school mates who had somehow leaned over an adjacent wall to pull me up into the crowd. Like my favourite National Football League player, Brett Favre of the Green Bay Packers, I was doing my own Lambeau Leap, Oz style. My boarding-school mates had painted their faces half in green and yellow for Australia and half in red for Canada. I was catapulted into their wild embraces and chants of "Aussie, Aussie, Aussie...Go, Canada!"

As startled Games officials pried me away from the happy melee and pulled me down, I continued on my dazed way to doping control, which was located inside the Opera House. I entered to a standing ovation from all the workers and volunteers inside. I was in such a state of excitement and confusion at this point that I thought, Who are they cheering for?

Suddenly it hit me.

They were cheering an Olympic champion.

GOLD MEDAL MOM

Parents can be emotional people, watching their kids play Pee Wee hockey or Little League baseball. So what's it like on the day for a mother to watch her child win a gold medal in the Olympic Games? My mom, Linda, went through a range of emotions on that day in Sydney. Here is the golden Olympic day as experienced by an anxious mom, in her words:

It was dark and cool coming in from Manly on race morning, moving toward the Olympic rings on the Sydney Harbour Bridge with the Opera House on the left and a full moon up on our right. Simon's sister Kate and I rushed to pick our seat in the stands. We were all on our own, away from the big Canadian contingent down at the finish line. The Opera House was now behind us and the bridge and the big screen were on our right.

I imagined Simon's dad, Geoff, pacing by himself outside the run/bike course, mentally taking Simon through his warm-ups and calming himself by reading a newly purchased book of poems by Michael Ondaatje.

Excitement built as the fifty competitors were introduced. We watched Simon squeezing his hands together, clapping his three good luck claps, getting the butterflies out.

I heard the countdown and hoped all was well out on the swim course, with all the thrashing arms and legs and cool choppy water. On sighting

Simon in the transition area after the swim, I thought to myself, He looks on track.

Looking at an empty number 18 bike stand, we knew Simon was now racing up Macquarie Street. I never did see him make that transition. And I missed him on the first two laps of the bike course. Finally I found him, and he was in eighth position!

It was going well—but then our hearts fell when his backside, with Whitfield clearly visible, flashed on the big screen and his feet were on the ground! That was the crash he survived.

Two bikers were already in the transition zone, and then thankfully, within seconds, a huge group came flying in. Simon was with them. And then the rush was on. He was twenty-fourth off the bike, but we soon saw him making his way by several of his competitors. I found him again on the far side and knew he had moved up, but now I worried about what he had left in the tank.

We had several sightings of him on the big screen, and then suddenly there he was running through transition zone in fourth place. Five kilometres to go. I thought to myself, Medal territory. Can he hold on? Where's Geoff?

Another shot of Simon on the big screen. He was coming down Macquarie and was looking good. Focused. I had not seen him look that good at the nine-and-a-half-kilometre mark.

Both leading runners came into view and the final dash unfolded before our eyes. Needless to say, we were a little noisy. Our friend Doug was yelling into the phone to his father, giving a play-by-play and video-taping at the same time. Lots of hugs. I almost lost my breath!

I watched Geoff making his way through the crowd and gate crashing. He didn't have a ticket, so he had to prove who he was. "That's my son that just won that!" he shouted. My sister, Janet Ames, and Simon's best friend, Jasper Blake, went to the far side of the big blue carpet and things got kind of emotional.

Then Simon St. Quentin Whitfield was kissing the podium and lifting his arms high in the air, his face in the flowers and the Canadian flag moving slowly up the pole. What happened next is a blur. We knew there was a ripple back in Canada. But when we arrived home to find a tidal wave had gone through, we were in awe. It seems the race was watched coast to coast.

The words Imagine the feeling had been spinning in Simon's head for a number of years. He will tell you that he imagined every part of that race, and right up to the finish-line tape, but nothing after that. Now the challenge became to balance life with visits to schools, corporate appearances, training and petting his cats.

THE RACING JERSEY

People have asked me if I was making some sort of fashion, or even political, statement with the front chest zipper being down on the Canadian racing suit I wore during the Sydney 2000 Summer Olympics race.

The answer is a simple and boring "No."

The darn thing was too snug, so I had to open the zipper to allow myself more room to move.

I didn't get the suit from Triathlon Canada officials until 8:00 PM the night before the race. They themselves had been waiting for its delivery.

"Looks like it fits," said Team Canada coach Barrie Shepley as I tried it on for the first time on the eve of the Olympic race.

"Well, it better fit, because there's not much we can do about it now," I replied.

So I put it back on the morning of the race and it felt great. In fact, I felt great.

What we didn't take into account was that it could shrink once I got out of the water. Sure enough the shoulders of the suit constricted as

I got on the bike, and suddenly my Olympic racing suit went from small to extra small. My only option was to open the front zipper as far as I could to give my shoulders room to move. My friend Ted gave me a hard time. No, I wasn't trying to show off my chest to impress the girls.

After I won the gold medal, one of the first questions a journalist asked in the media scrum was if the zipper being down was to symbolically show "the split" between English and French Canada, with one red side of the suit representing English Canada and the other French Canada and the unzipped zipper representing some sort of split.

"Huh? What?" I replied in astonishment.

It was my first experience with a ridiculous question from the media.

It wasn't long before I got my second.

Another journalist asked me if my bare chest meant that I considered myself "the ultimate showman."

"No," I replied again.

I had no other uniform and no other option after the shoulders of the suit shrunk and became tight in the water.

They say things come in threes, and the third bizarre question in the media scrum after I crossed the line first in Sydney that day was whether I had taken the finish-line banner and tossed it down to the ground "to show displeasure at the International Olympic Committee and in defiance of the IOC."

"What?" I sputtered back, again in disbelief at the query. "Why would I do that?"

I had no beef against the IOC. I was just so happy and ecstatic and shocked to be the Olympic champion, so I grabbed the banner and threw it to the ground in jubilation.

Strange suit. Strange questions. An exciting day, indeed.

CHAPTER 2

Growing Up

I grew up in Kingston, Ontario, Canada, near the Queen's University campus. We used to laughingly, and lovingly, refer to the area as the Ghetto of Queen's. Every night my friends would call and we would go out to play pickup sports. It was a tight-knit neighbourhood with a tight-knit group of friends, who all lived in a four- to six-block radius. This was definitely not the suburbs but a true city neighbourhood, and we all remember it fondly. Within those city blocks, which included both my own Victoria Public School and Winston Churchill School, was our entire world.

Several friends from my growing-up years—Ted Jennings, Adrian Leslie and Jesse Ohtake—started off in Montessori together and remain friends for life. Jesse was a very quiet and incredibly thoughtful kid. So obviously Jesse went on to become what else but a hip-hop producer in Toronto! Ted works on Bay Street in Toronto's financial district. He was a line manager at Chrysler at age twenty-three and now works in banking. Ted has attended all my Olympic races, from Sydney to Athens to Beijing.

I grew up with a great group of friends in Kingston, Ontario. Kris Carrier, Ted Jennings, Nick Thorne and I (L-R) hamming it up for the camera at a soccer game.

We categorized everyone when we were youngsters. I thought of Ted as "Calculator Boy," because he would always have to get his homework done before coming out to play and was always the young banker and a born leader who lead with action ahead of talk. "Free Spirit" was Adrian Leslie, who went on to live far and wide and was with me during my golden moment in Sydney.

We played on the Chalmers Church hockey teams, although my friends were more serious about Canada's passion—that being hockey, not church—than I was. Soccer was my true passion, and it was the sport I most avidly played while growing up. The interactions learned in team sports have perhaps set me apart in the world of individual sports such as triathlon. I came to respect the value of teamwork, even as it applies in the context of an individual race. That's why I've always liked to work in tight training groups in Victoria with people with whom I am close and comfortable. Maybe this background explains why I pushed for the idea of a Canadian team approach as we prepared for the Beijing 2008 Summer Olympics.

Now an admission I hope doesn't make me sound too weird or geeky. As a youngster I was one of those closet nerds who was totally into Dungeons & Dragons. And I mean seriously into it until grade eight. The group I got involved with, which was largely outside my regular circle of friends, spent endless hours at the game and built the most complex worlds you could imagine. It got to the point I started doing terribly at school and became a straight-C student. While my friends outside the game circle were getting As, all I wanted to do was play Dungeons & Dragons at night and soccer during the day. I was obsessed with the puzzles the game presented and loved its creative spirit.

Looking back, this obsession with a board game perhaps offers a bit of a key to my personality to this day. When I'm obsessed with something, I'm relentless in pursuing it. I once got so immersed in a game of pickup football that I spent nearly five hours straight playing it with a group of guys I wouldn't allow to leave until my side finally won. Because I always insisted that the victor has to "win by two," the game could be virtually endless. If my team scored the go-ahead goal, I would slack off to get it back to even, and the game would just have to continue.

TRIATHLON 101

OLYMPIC DISTANCE: 1.5 kilometre swim; 40 kilometre bike ride; 10 kilometre run.
HALF IRON DISTANCE: 1.9 kilometre swim; 90 kilometre bike ride; 21.09 kilometre run.
IRONMAN DISTANCE: 3.8 kilometre swim; 180 kilometre bike ride; 42.2 kilometre run.
KIDS OF STEEL and IRONKIDS: (Distances vary with age group): 100 to 750 metre swim; 5 to 15 kilometre bike ride; 1 to 5 kilometre run.

I wish I could have done better at school. My sister Kate, now an engineer and city planner in Ottawa, was very much my opposite in that regard. She was athletic and rowed at the Canadian high-school championship level, but she also did well in school. It was sports that became my vehicle to grab attention.

My friends and I attended Kingston Collegiate high school, where I made myself proud by making the school's powerful basketball team.

I made the team but was the kid who got the water bottles for the other players and the one who gave the high fives when they came off the floor. I was the player they would send out with twenty-six seconds remaining in a blowout game. I remember that I hit one three-pointer—the highlight of my hoops career. But the team was so good—an Eastern Cities regional power—that it remains a source of pride to this very day that I was able to crack the lineup, albeit on the end of the bench with my good friend, Jay Pierce.

It was through soccer that I really discovered how fast I could run. That led me to joining my high-school cross-country team, where, perhaps not to my complete surprise, I won many of the Eastern Cities regional high-school races. I was a bit undersized but could feel my speed emerging. My events on the track were the 800 metres and 1,500 metres. I took fourth place in both of these at the Ontario high-school track and field championships in my grade-ten year. The other runners were physically more mature in terms of musculature and such, but I realized that I could get better as my body also matured.

It was then that a strange new sport—a combination of swimming, cycling and running—began to gain in popularity. Once the domain of kooks and outsiders, triathlon was making inroads into the popular sporting culture and races were being held in the lake country of Ontario. It intrigued me. Heck, I knew how to swim and ride a bike and

I loved cross-country running when I was a kid. It took agility and heart to run fast. I certainly didn't always win (third place here), but I loved being on the team. To this day, when I'm on a bus or a plane, I can stare out the window and picture myself running along some familiar trail, just as I did as a kid on the way to meets.

was developing into a pretty decent runner, known for an extremely relaxed running style. How hard could it be?

Always up for a new sporting hurdle, I got the chance through my friend Brandon. His parents, Rudy and Joan, organized the Sharbot Lake Triathlon. They owned a cottage on the lake, and we spent endless summer days there. I decided to embark on a challenge. It was essentially a bet that Brandon and I took with his dad that we could finish a triathlon. It was 1986 but I recall that first race like it was yesterday. I barely survived the swim and then rode my rather cumbersome mountain bike as fast as I could. I completed the running portion in my boxer shorts—which had cow designs—to cover up those crazy small swimming trunks we wore. I finished, but well back in the field. But I finished. That was the important thing. And perhaps more

My wonderful sister (left) and her best friend, Alison Thorne, joined me at a local Kids of Steel triathlon. We travelled around Ontario in the summer, racing and camping almost every weekend. We were very lucky to have such supportive parents.

important still, I absolutely loved it and couldn't wait to do it all again. Who could have imagined back then what the outcome would be of that decision?

My passion for the sport was immediately born, and thoughts of triathlon began to dominate my daily routine. I immediately recognized the need to improve my swimming and asked my parents if I could join the Blue Marlins Swim Club for winter lessons.

On the track at Richardson Stadium in Kingston, Ontario. I ran the 800, 1,500 and 3,000 metre for Kingston Collegiate. I sure was a skinny kid—no football team for me.

After five years of racing on the Ontario Kids of Steel circuit, I was having moderate success in the local races. That led to the decision to race at the 1992 Canadian Junior Triathlon Championships at Kelowna, British Columbia. I placed a respectable sixteenth overall in my first truly national race. And it hit me. I can do this, and I might actually be decent at it. Nobody was talking Olympic glory, of course, but it seemed I had at least found an interesting sporting path.

It's too bad I wasn't as scholastically oriented as I was athletically. This became a concern for my dad. In the midst of my grade-eleven year, I had an idea and a suggestion. It was rather daring and audacious—at least in the mind of a teen who would have to leave hearth, home, family, school and friends—and involved my dad's old school in Australia. My friends couldn't believe I wouldn't be part of graduation ceremonies with them the following year. Mom cried her eyes out at the Toronto airport. My cross-Pacific schooling adventure was about to begin.

BUMPY EARLY RACES

Olympic careers emerge from the most unlikely of beginnings. I am a prime example. Even if your results are not there early on, never give up. Be persistent. You never know where it could lead. And always be prepared, at any level of sport.

There was the time my Aunt Janet took on parenting duties at a triathlon far from home in Surrey, British Columbia. Brandon Hollywood and I were sixteen years old and out to gain racing experience with other up-and-coming junior triathletes. Race preparations went well, and everybody gathered down at the water's edge for the start of the race.

Aunt Janet took one last look at my bike in the transition area. She noticed immediately the helmet was missing. The last time she had seen it, it had been in the trunk of the car, which was now some distance away. Aunt Janet thought a moment of letting me learn from my mistake. But, of course, she ran to the car for the forgotten helmet.

And, when arriving at my bike, grabbing my helmet, did I give a quick thought to my having put it there before the race? No. But the stand-in parenting part was done, thanks to Aunt Janet. And the lesson was learned later in the telling of what happened.

There was another lesson learned in an early race when competing in the Smith Falls Annual Triathlon in Ontario as a kid. I had made my way down to the start line, without a backward look at my bike waiting in the transition zone. My mother, however, could see the chain had come off the bike. The race began and I had a good swim. But what would happen in the bike transition? I still didn't know the chain needed to be fixed.

"I chose to stand back, actually behind a tree, to watch how Simon was going to deal with the situation," recalls my mom. "I can report that there was indeed a moment of 'Errgh!' Fortunately, there was nothing

I would call 'blue language.' Simon got to the task of putting the chain back on and was quickly back in the race, greasy hands and all."

And it was another lesson learned about not taking equipment for granted and not letting race hiccups early in your sports career derail you from your goals.

FAVOURITE TEACHER

I had many dedicated and inspiring teachers while growing up. A good teacher, like a good coach, can inspire and raise you to greater heights of personal development. The teacher who really stands out for me is George Turcotte, my social studies and history teacher in grades eight and nine. If we were studying Rome, the whole class would be made up to resemble the Roman Coliseum. When we studied World War II, our classroom was made up to resemble a bunker so we could almost feel what the soldiers went through. Mr. Turcotte was so passionate and creative that he instilled an interest in history, and the world, that has stayed with me to this day.

Because the school board could only purchase prescribed books for classrooms, Mr. Turcotte would buy his own books that he thought would be of interest to the class. Because of that, I was introduced to a wide range of books at an early age that have influenced and stayed with me—particularly *Dolphin Crossing* and challenging fare such as *Ulysses* and *All Quiet on the Western Front*. We even learned calligraphy in Mr. Turcotte's class! He let us be creative. And that is what great teaching is all about.

CHAPTER 3
Sydney: The First Time Around

That I ended up in Australia to complete my high school years may seem strange to Canadians. I wanted to be the best at something in sports, and I knew Australians were the best at whatever they tried in terms of physical activity. I thought some of it could rub off on me.

Dad listened intently, as is his nature, when I first brought it up. He then made it happen. When he approached me about it six months after I had first mentioned Australia, I had almost forgotten about that idea. But things were not going well in terms of high school in Kingston, and I needed a jolt of some kind in my life. Dad, following up my earlier musings about Australia, suggested Oz could provide that kick-start.

"But do you want to leave home, family and lifelong friends, not to mention Canada, to do this...in the middle of your grade-eleven year?"

I steadied myself.

"Yes, Dad. I'm serious."

It was Christmas of 1992. If I left soon, I could make it in time for the second semester of the Australian school year, which began in January.

My dad, who attended Knox Grammar School when growing up, looked up from his newspaper. He knew how much I loved running and that I was burning inside to be good.

But Australia?

Even if it was at his old school.

He promised to look into it.

My dad and Knox Grammar School headmaster, Dr. Patterson, were old friends from their days together at the University of Alberta science department. As a couple of Aussie students in a fellow Commonwealth nation, but an otherwise strange, cold and snowy land, they naturally bonded as friends.

Now, these many years later, my dad made a call to his old friend.

I was national level in Canada but nothing really special. The previous August, I had placed sixteenth at the National Junior Triathlon Championships in Kelowna. It was okay, but hardly the stuff of world beaters.

But my dad's old connection proved key, and suddenly I was saying good-bye to all my old friends and school mates from Kingston and flying across Canada and the Pacific Ocean alone to a place I had only imagined in my dreams. I had left home and hearth in Kingston and come halfway around the world to Australia to the Knox Grammar School in the northern Sydney suburb of Taramara—my dad's hometown.

I didn't get off to a good start to my Aussie years.

My dad had drawn me a map, indicating the way to the school from the Sydney airport, but I got off the train at the wrong transfer point. There I was, clutching two suitcases and standing at the Circular Quay Station, about two hundred metres from the Opera House on Sydney Harbour. I certainly could not have imagined then the huge role this particular part of the city would play in my life eight years later. For now, I was in a strange large city in a strange new land, and if I wasn't careful I was about to start crying my eyes out.

I remember so vividly to this day wondering, What have I done? What have I gotten myself into?

I finally got the directions straightened out and soon a train had transported me to the lush and impressive campus of Knox Grammar School in the far northern suburbs of Sydney. This was a train I would ride almost daily for the next four years, back and forth from school, to the triathlon club, to races and to see friends.

I was the first student to arrive by a couple of days and stayed alone in the boarding house my first couple of nights. Wandering the halls of Ewan House and reading up on the rich history of this incredible school was an experience in itself. Knox had produced a number of legendary athletes, from rugby captains to Olympic swimmers.

Two days after arrival, I ventured to the pool to meet Chuck Atkins, the school's swim coach and my taskmaster over the next two years. As I walked up the school drive, past the church, business centre and the headmaster's house, I found myself walking with James Edwards. "Eddie" was the first student I came across. He would go on to be the swim-team captain and my informal swim advisor. Eddie was a typical

Knox Grammar School, 1992. I actually liked wearing the school uniform, complete with blue blazer and straw "boater." I earned my letters and a silver thistle by winning 32 of 32 races for the school over the two years I was there.

swimmer with a solid build, crazy chlorine-burned hair and a smile that seemed as big as the ocean that separated me from home.

On that first day he was wearing a blue blazer with the school insignia emblazoned on the breast pocket, the school tie and khaki shorts. Suddenly, it hit me that private school in Australia was going to be vastly different than public school in Canada, where jeans and running shoes were the unofficial dress code. The odd thing was that

Eddie was also wearing a Dallas Cowboys cap. I had come to the land of cricket, swimming, Aussie-rules football and rugby only to see a kid in a Cowboys cap. That, of course, was an instant conversation starter and James Edwards became my first friend at Knox Grammar School and, over the course of my stay, one of my best mates at school.

TRIATHLON 101

TRANSITION AREAS: *Yes, the time it takes to get out of the water and onto the bike and off the bike and into your running shoes counts in the overall timing of a triathlon race. So be quick through the transitions, or it will cost you valuable time.*

He led me to the pool, where I was introduced to the members of the school swim team, none of whom could stop staring at me and asking if everyone in Canada was so white and pasty.

It was a couple weeks later that I was led to Dr. Patterson's office. I arrived early and waited outside his office and had an instant crush on his secretary. Her accent and Aussie style was mesmerizing to a pasty-faced Canadian. I pretended to look through a book on the history of Knox School, while trying not to be caught staring at her. She turned out to be the wife of my social-studies teacher. I obviously then never liked him.

I was soon ushered in to see the headmaster. Dr. Patterson was a commanding man—tall, angular and athletic. His office, all mahogany and dark leathers, was something out of *Tom Brown's School Days*. It was sort of what I always imagined the Prime Minister's office to be.

And here I was, a skinny Canadian transplant, standing in his office alone, afraid and unsure. Dr. Patterson got right to the point. He said my home dorm would be Ewan House (of which I would eventually become vice-captain along with an incredible rugby player named Jonny Straton). Dr. Patterson informed me he really wasn't all that interested in my triathlon and swimming ambitions, but that

I could take part in both as long as they didn't affect my studies and my running.

Since I was essentially an "unofficial" athletic-scholarship student, apparently certain things were expected of me. But I almost choked on my chewing gum when Dr. Patterson said he expected me to become city champion in running and break all of the school's middle-distance records by the time I graduated in two years. He never flinched or smiled. He was dead serious.

I left the meeting and found a pay phone in the hall and phoned my dad collect. It was 2:00 AM back in Kingston.

"Dad, you won't believe what the headmaster just told me," I said, many thousands of kilometres and a culture away from my comfort zone.

"They expect me to be city champion and break all the schools records."

Silence.

Then my dad said, "Well, then break them."

TRIATHLON 101

THE BOSSES: *International Triathlon Union (ITU) for Olympic distance, and World Triathlon Corporation (WTC) for Ironman.*

I was shocked and just stared at the phone. I then looked up and down the hall to make sure no one was coming, as I felt like I could burst into tears at any moment. I responded, "Excuse me, Dad, I thought you would be appalled and would want to call Dr. Patterson and tell him not to put so much pressure on me."

I was starting to learn this was going to be tough love. No dream comes easy. And Dr. Patterson and my father were conspiring to teach me the demanding Aussie way. These people set their bars high and take no prisoners in sports, and that's probably why they produce so many Olympic champions. And wasn't that what I wanted to be, even if I had yet to dare to admit such a foolishly lofty goal?

But it wasn't an auspicious start to this part of my journey.

"Mom and I will love you no matter what," Dad continued. "It's all a matter of dedication and commitment, son. If you commit yourself, make the sacrifices and always put in the best effort you can, then results will take care of themselves. I'm repeating myself here but your family will always love and support you. But if you want to be an athlete, and a good one, this is the kind of pressure you will be under."

Gee, thanks, Dad! Nevertheless, I realized those were sage words. And they clicked. I immediately got it and clearly understood everything he was saying.

The alarm clock rang as 5:30 AM came much too early the next day. In terms of getting up in the morning, I have a ten-second rule, and I've never broken it. No matter how tired I am, no matter how much I want to sleep in, if I start counting to ten, I always get out of bed at the count of nine. I say to myself, "Is this the morning, after all this time, after all those mornings, that you want to finally break the ten-second rule?" I have never once slept in on my ten-second rule, although there have been a couple mornings I simply never started counting.

Bleary-eyed, I made my way to the school pool. Typical of the Aussies' love of swimming, and their cultural history of brilliance in the water, the Knox School pool would make the grade as a first-rate municipal pool in any city in Canada. In Australia, it's just another school pool. Sydney has forty-eight Olympic-size pools. Toronto has three. Australia is a country completely surrounded by water and there's something about that mythic fact that has turned Aussies into a nation of swimmers. They swim like Canadians play hockey.

"Are you the new kid?" shouted the coach in charge.

"Sixteen-year-olds are in lane six."

So I went to lane six and jumped in. And promptly got lapped by just about every other sixteen-year-old in the Knox School swim program.

Coach Atkins was not impressed.

"Move over one lane and see how you do against the fifteen-year-olds," he said, with a growing frown.

Again, smoked.

"Move over one more lane," said Coach Atkins with growing alarm.

By the time this humiliating lane-jumping was over, I was swimming with the twelve-year-old girls from the neighbouring all-female Pymbel School.

And I couldn't even beat them.

I had been thinking of getting a Maple Leaf tattoo put on my chest before I left Canada. Now, I was so glad I didn't. I would have embarrassed my entire nation in the eyes of Knox Grammar School swimming.

Oddly enough, that day, and for my remaining days at Knox School, the other students starting calling me "Yank." Normally, for a Canadian, that would be considered the ultimate insult. But, swimming with the twelve-year-old girls, I didn't mind and was actually sort of relieved that many of my fellow students thought I was American. It's a Super Power. It could stand a little misplaced embarrassment courtesy of a sixteen-year-old wannabe world-class athlete who couldn't even keep up with a bunch of twelve-year-old girls.

FAVE RAVE—SWIMMING, CYCLING OR RUNNING?

Triathlon is a unique sport in that it is actually an amalgam of three sports—swimming, cycling and running. Fans often wonder which of the three is a triathlete's favourite. The answer, of course, varies with each different triathlete. A triathlete who came to our sport from a cycling background is likely to pick that as his or her favourite part of the race. Someone who comes from swimming is, of course, likely to pick that.

Although I came to triathlon primarily from a running background, I find cycling the most interesting of triathlon's three components. That's because cyclists tend to be the most scientifically knowledgeable about their sport. Perhaps it's because I like to keep it simple—and running is the simplest form of human movement—that I find the complexities of cycling to be all that more intriguing. It could be a question of opposites attracting. So I spend the most time picking the brains of cyclists for tips and clues, not swimmers or runners. It is not an insult to the other two sports, but compared to the best runner and best swimmer, you'll find that the cyclist is the most sophisticated athlete of the three. That's why I like talking to them the most.

I do so much love the purity and simplicity of swimming and running. Cycling is that too, but with a layer of complexity added, because you are dealing with a machine on which you ride. You must know about the mechanics of that machine if you are to be successful. But it's one-third of what we do, and generally my training concentrates 33 percent on each discipline.

Each stage has its own unique challenges and nuances in the whole of a triathlon race. You can't win a race with your swimming, but you can lose it. You can lose it even more on the bike if you lose contact with the lead pack. Triathlon finishes with a run, so that obviously is of utmost importance. Having a strong kick down the stretch drive is one of the main keys to our sport. That's why I'm glad I came to triathlon from a running background and that it is the strongest part of my game.

A DAD'S PERSPECTIVE

My dad, Geoff, has been quietly yet so profoundly influential on my life and career and that of my sister Kate. Nobody goes out specifically to raise an Olympian. But it doesn't hurt to have a support at home. I had that in spades with both my mom and dad. Here are my dad's thoughts:

What might have influenced the development of Simon and Kate positively has been focused on the importance of the theme:

"Assist them to develop spirit and resilience and a command of the English language; the rest will take care of itself." A bit of luck is essential; this may amount to nothing more than the absence of bad luck.

Central to attaining "spirit and resilience" is the development of self-esteem—but not self-importance. Spirit and resilience takes the application of imagination and intelligence, so that forming synapses is key. Intelligence is accomplished as much by exposure to a wide range of activities that are connected to a child's gifts—whatever these may be—as it is by formal education. Imagination is something that one hopes can be kept alive as a child is necessarily exposed to society's demands.

It is essential to have the capacity to communicate. Taking in the ideas of others is key; visualizing is key.

Two important outcomes of developing spirit and resilience: Both Simon and Kate can compete, and both are prudent risk-takers.

Simon's Scrapbook: The Early Years

Ted and me being Ted and me

Taking the plunge!

Mom teaches me the moves

Contemplating my future career in hockey...

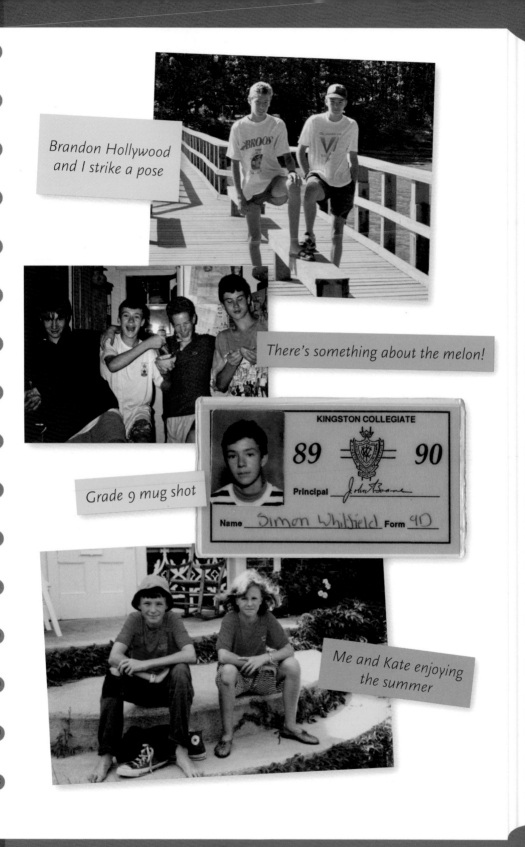

Brandon Hollywood and I strike a pose

There's something about the melon!

KINGSTON COLLEGIATE

89 = 90

Principal *John Boone*

Name *Simon Whitfield* Form 9D

Grade 9 mug shot

Me and Kate enjoying the summer

CHAPTER 4
School Of Hard Knox

I quickly got into the routine of preppy Australian school life—early morning swim lessons followed by classes—even though I thought I looked skinny and geekish in the school blazer and shorts. I was never proud of my knobby knees, and being in shorts every waking minute didn't help matters.

Perhaps there is something in the Aussie character that makes them so competitive. Knox held numerous school track meets on a grass track, and the entire student population was compelled to attend to see who the fastest students were from month to month. Even many of the old boys would return to campus for some of the bigger meets. It was something of a tradition.

And yes, it became apparent soon enough that Dr. Patterson had not asked me to shoot for anything unattainable. I broke the records and became school champion in the 800 metre and 1,500 metre. His prediction of city championships couldn't be far behind.

Another great sporting tradition at Knox was the Aquaton races—a four-hundred-metre swim in the school pool, followed by a two-kilometre run—and every student was expected to compete. I remember

The Combined Associated Schools track meet in my senior year at high school saw our team win, and I fulfilled my promise to the headmaster by winning the 1,500 and the 3,000 metre. My schoolmates were in the stands chanting "O Canada!", just as they did six years later and a few kilometres away on the steps of the Sydney Opera House. That's me, second from left.

there was a large boy who said he couldn't. They still made him. The pool was shallow at one end, so he defiantly walked his four hundred metres there instead of swimming and then he walked the two kilometres of the run. Good on him, I thought to myself.

Another boy named Dave, however, was at the opposite end of the spectrum. He had so often been school champion for each of his grades that people stopped counting. Since he was a day boy, all the day boys had lined the course to cheer on Dave. By this point, I had grown somewhat stronger and more confident, and my natural abilities were coming to the fore. I had (thankfully) left the twelve-year-old girls in my wake. My acceleration was rapid and I was really coming on as an athlete, and word was starting to spread throughout the school. All the boarding students had also lined the course in support of me. An intense rivalry between day boys and boarders is a pretty standard fact of life at private schools everywhere. Both sets of supporters were in full throaty roar as Dave and I set out at the head of the pack.

Dave's winning streak ended that day; he would not be the champion of grade eleven. I caught him with two hundred metres to go in the run and never looked back. Knox School had a new Aquaton champion, and the boarders roared their approval. Maybe I wasn't too bad an athlete, after all.

People ask me why I am the way I am. If I see a challenge, I don't back off. It's not in me not to meet an obstacle head-on and try to defeat it. And that's what led to perhaps my greatest achievement at Knox School—the vanquishing of the school bully.

From the first day I arrived, I knew I didn't like him. He was a large boy—his name will go unmentioned—and he picked on more vulnerable members of our student body, as bullies always do. Everyone was too afraid to stand up to him. Ever since I was a little boy, I've detested bullies. I simply can't stand it when the strong pick on the weak.

My personal introduction to the Knox School bully came in social-studies class in just my second week at the school. I was about to hand in my assignment when the bully, sitting next to me, grabbed it out of my hand and rubbed my name off it and put his name on and handed it in to the teacher as his completed assignment.

You couldn't make this up. It was surreal, like something out of one of those old John Hughes teen movies—Aussie edition.

"What are you going to do about it, sissy Yank?" he said with a menacing laugh.

I have always been slight but feisty, and so I shoved him, asking what he thought he was doing. He shoved back. Harder. I was on my back, with the teacher shouting at both of us. What an introduction to the Australian schooling system in just my second week!

After that, the bully antagonized me for my entire time at Knox School. Until the final day of school. In one class, we were asked to write an inspiring phrase on the blackboard, summing up our time at Knox. I had just returned to my seat, when I noticed the bully had gone up and wiped clean what I had written and then laughed.

I don't know what got into me, but I had had enough. I'm not a fighter, but he could not go unchallenged. Not on the last day of school. Even though I would probably never see him again, I knew then and

I should be wearing a helmet. Still to this day, when I get a new bike, I take it out of for a lap of the block, and I feel like a kid on Cooper Street whipping around the block being chased by Ted.

there it was my time and place to take a stand. I did. And I cleaned his clock, while every other student in the class let out years of pent-up frustration and cheered me on lustily.

The bully was much bigger than me, but I was more wiry and athletic. I wasn't thinking of that specifically at the time, but there was probably a message in that somewhere for me. It's not the size of the dog in the fight, but the size of the fight in the dog. And on that day I had a lot of fight in me, and the big, cowering former bully now knew it.

Now, how to channel that in positive ways?

In my grade-twelve year, I moved out of Ewan House and took a one-bedroom apartment near the campus behind the Hornsby Subway Station on Bobbin Head Road. It was near Galston Gorge, a popular running track, so that was fine by me. In my mind, I had renamed it *Kenyan Trail*, dreaming of one day running like the Kenyans.

I was reading a lot of triathlon books by this time—Ironman legend Dave Scott's *Triathlon Training* was a particular favourite—in an attempt to feed my mind as well as my body with knowledge about an emerging new sport that was starting to seriously intrigue me. I was good at running but not yet great. I was only okay at swimming and could see no future in that as a stand-alone event. I had always enjoyed cycling back around the old neighbourhood in Kingston and proved quite fast when first encouraged to join an official club.

At one discipline, I was unlikely to become a world-class athlete, although running was my best option. But combining swimming, cycling and running got me thinking.

Also at that time, I was becoming immersed in all things Australian. In fact, at that point, I wanted to be Australian and compete for Australia internationally if I ever reached that level. Because of my father's Australian birth, that could have been a possibility for me. I had yet to discover what it truly meant to be Canadian. I was, however, discovering what it meant to be a triathlete.

I joined the Balmoral Triathlon Club in 1993, after racing at the Port Macquarie Triathlon Club, and began immersing myself in the sport. A young, then unheard-of triathlete named Greg Bennett was also a club member. I was committed, but I was still Simon.

TRIATHLON 101

FAMOUS TRIATHLON RACES: *Quadrennial: Summer Olympics, Commonwealth Games, Pan American Games, Asian Games; Annual: Hawaii Ironman World Championship, Escape from Alcatraz, Wildflower Half Iron, World Cup Des Moines, Ironman Germany, Ironman Canada, Ironman Australia, Ironman New Zealand, Ironman Lanzarote, ITU Triathlon (Olympic Distance) World Championship.*

After all those days of 5:30-AM swim sessions in the Knox School pool, I thought it was kind of cool to be able to sleep in when school ended. I admit I'm not always the most super-organized guy in the world. It was Greg who would pick me up for races, thus ensuring I was ready to go. If one of the great up-and-comers of the sport was outside my door beeping the horn at 6:00 AM, who was I to blow off training and stay under the covers and go back to sleep?

So while most of my graduating classmates were up at Surfer's Paradise for Schoolies Week—a students-gone-wild Aussie graduation-

Greg Bennett is like my big brother, and this photo hangs in our living room. He taught me everything he knew. I was his understudy and can't thank him enough.

week tradition that makes Fort Lauderdale look like kindergarten—I stayed home because I had a triathlon race. When it came to racing, I have always known to have the proper priorities.

I won a big race that year in Penrith, but the rest of the time I just kept getting hammered, placing well back in race after race. I hate losing, yet I wasn't discouraged. I simply became more determined. Greg and I would go on endless training rides across town, over the Sydney Harbour Bridge out to Manly Beach and all over that vast but spectacular metropolis.

The graduation ceremonies for the Knox School class of 1994 were held on the steps of the Sydney Opera House. A year earlier, I had joined thousands of others there in celebration as we watched on

Nana, my dad's mother, was an incredible woman. I remember how proud she was when I graduated Knox Grammar School some forty years after my father. I think I get my relentless drive from her, which she showed throughout her entire life.

a jumbo screen as International Olympic Committee then-president Juan Antonio Samaranch had opened an envelope and announced, "The 2000 Olympic Summer Games have been awarded to the city of...Sydney." I didn't hear much more after that as the massive throng erupted. Only later would we learn the vote was razor thin, 45–43, for Sydney over Beijing on the last ballot.

Triathlon had been voted into the Summer Olympics earlier and was set to join the Games roster of sports in 2000. I sat on the steps of the Opera House that day, watching the wild celebratory scenes unfold, and then I said to myself, "Okay, triathlon is going to be my job."

Little could I have imagined then the Olympian fate which awaited me at the finish line—right there directly by the steps of the Sydney Opera House—in six years' time.

MOST INSPIRING BOOK AND MOVIE

My favourite book, and the one that has inspired me the most in my life, is *The Power of One* by Bryce Courtenay. It tells the tale of an English boy named Peekay growing up in South Africa. How much has this book influenced me? Well, my daughter's name is PK, short for Pippa Kathryn. Peekay to PK. There's a reason for that.

I was about fourteen or fifteen when the book first came out, and it had an immediate impact on me. I find *The Power of One* to be incredibly uplifting in how it details the life of a child who is an outsider, English-speaking Peekay, who is sent to an Afrikaner school and humiliated and ostracized by the staff and other students. The story chronicles how one child—the power of one!—has the ability to change his own circum-stances with the support of a colourful group of characters who come into his life. Peekay overcomes the setbacks in life and rises above all the hatred. One of the tools Peekay utilizes is boxing—a central focus of the story. There is a metaphor in this tale for all young people in sports. I know there is for me.

My favourite movie is *The Great Escape*, with Steve McQueen and many other great actors from the 1960s, and was made before I was even born. What really draws me to this film is a sense of marvel over just how resourceful these men were as they strived again and again to escape from a German prisoner-of-war camp during World War II and how their spirit couldn't be broken. They were resilient. They kept going and going and going and trying and trying and trying. They were simply relentless. I can see why this is my favourite movie and why I find it so inspiring. Resourcefulness, spirit, resilience, relentlessness and the drive and desire to keep going and trying are all the things which go into making a great athlete.

Simon's Scrapbook: First Competitions

Ontario Track and Field Championships

Cross-country running

Mom and Kate with me as I prepare for my first race against older competitors

Pedals to the metal with Brandon Hollywood

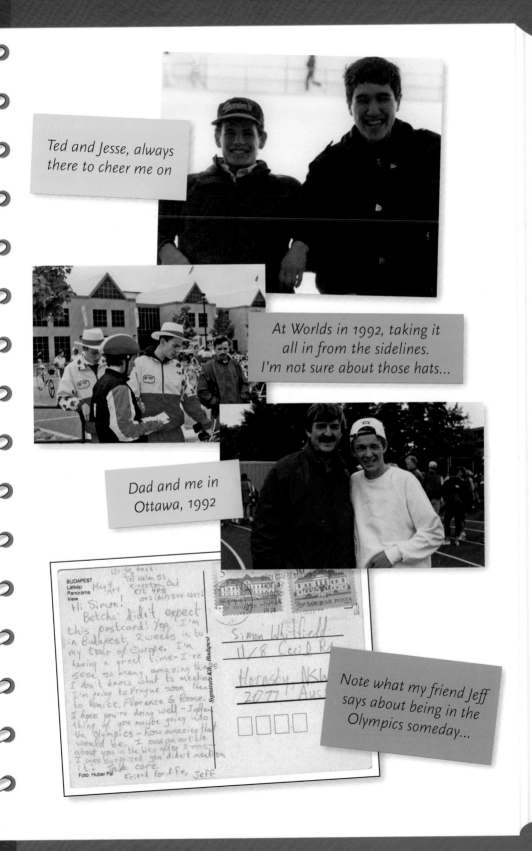

Ted and Jesse, always there to cheer me on

At Worlds in 1992, taking it all in from the sidelines. I'm not sure about those hats...

Dad and me in Ottawa, 1992

Note what my friend Jeff says about being in the Olympics someday...

CHAPTER 5

Growing Pains

After graduation, I didn't continue on to university, college or technical school, or get a job like many young people after grade twelve. Well, actually I did take a job—that of a pro triathlete. I had made a promise to myself on the steps of the Sydney Opera House and was going to keep it.

My physical maturation kept apace, enough to get me noticed in triathlon circles. Nobody was mapping out parade routes for me yet, but at least I was now on the radar. After graduation in 1994, I was invited for a series of workouts and tests in a talent identification camp at the famed Australian Institute of Sport. Full of myself, I laid into the bike and was determined to show off my ability. The lab guys seemed suitably impressed as they looked at each other and wrote what I assumed were laudatory notes. Then it was on to the treadmill and even more raised eyebrows.

"You're awesome, mate. These are great results. Better than all the others," said one guy in a white coat as he scribbled furiously.

I don't know why I thought this, but I did. I smiled smugly and thought to myself that they were saying my treadmill results were better than anybody's they had ever seen—which must have meant that they were better than Aussie marathon legends Rob de Castella and Steve Moneghetti, whose pictures prominently adorned the walls of the training room. I immedi-ately thought: Great! I'm crushing these guys' results. I'm on my way to world sporting greatness, just like Rob and Steve. And it didn't even take that long for me to get there.

TRIATHLON 101

THE CRAZIEST RACE I'VE EVER DONE: *The French Iron Tour—eight races in nine days, almost all Olympic distance. It is the Tour de France of triathlon.*

When I foolishly let a version of these thoughts slip to the lab technicians running the tests, the gales of laughter reverberated out of the AIS building, and I'm sure all the way back across the Pacific to Canada.

"Rob de Castella and Steve Moneghetti? You testing better than them? What the hell are you talking about, mate? Dream on. That's not what we meant. We meant you were testing better than the other kids your age."

Ah yes, welcome back to planet Earth...Still, that was obviously good news. But as for the skinny eighteen-year-old thinking he had suddenly arrived as the world's next great triathlete, well, I will never *ever* forget the roaring waves of laughter that filled that room.

After that I promptly went out and got clobbered in just about every race I ran as a junior during the rest of 1994. If I was on the road to de Castella- and Moneghetti-like international sporting status, I sure had a strange way of showing it.

By 1995, however, the results started coming. I placed fourth in the Australian Junior Championships, won the Canadian Juniors and recorded a breakthrough tenth-place finish at the World Junior Championships in Cancun, Mexico.

And it was about this time that my Canadian genes started kicking in. I began leaning away from the idea of representing Australia,

My first World Championship in Cancun, Mexico, in 1995. I remember all I wanted to do was see Simon Lessing from Great Britain, my triathlon hero.

if I ever got good enough to be a serious international athlete. In fact, I began to look forward to finding a way to stick it to the Aussies. I enjoyed my four years in Oz, and their feisty competitiveness was in line with my own. But, truth be told, I was Canadian. And I began feeling more acutely Canadian the longer I stayed away. Surrounded by Aussies, it became obvious to me I wasn't one of them. I was a Canuck through and through. This was a feeling that grew within me. When you know, you just know. I knew I could never wear the green and gold of Australia. I was red and white all over, and those were the colours that most represented me and who I was. And those would be the colours in which I would race.

The first chance came as a twenty-year-old at the 1996 World Championships in Cleveland. But my first senior World Championship race was not a happy occasion. Far from it. It was simple, Simon: I just didn't have it that day. It happens in all sports. It happens in triathlon, and it happened to me. Welcome to the big leagues, kid. Now get out of the way before you get run over. That is the ultimate insult to a triathlete. If you are lapped in a World Championship or World Cup race, you are automatically disqualified. I was in real danger of having that happen to me in my first World Championship. What an impressive debut that would be! Yet just before I was lapped, and on the bike portion to really rub it in, I heard a tire pop. I could feel the leaders beginning to bear down on me as I thought to myself, Oh, please, let that flat tire be mine.

Luckily, it was. My flat enabled me to pull out of the race with a "Did Not Finish" and so saved myself the ignominy of being lapped and being disqualified in my first world championship. DNFs are never good, but sometimes they can prove opportune. That one did for me.

The next year it was back down to a familiar land, and I finished ninth at the 1997 World Championships in Perth, Australia. That was absolutely huge for me. With Sydney 2000 three years away, I made the kind of breakthrough needed to prove I was serious about competing in the Olympics. After all, ninth is not the best but it's a hugely respectable slot for a twenty-one-year-old to be occupying. And it sure beats being lapped or not finishing!

Another big result in 1997 was over the summer in the Iron Tour, a gruelling eight-races-in-nine-days throughout France. I remember it for so many reasons, none of which was more important than the $4,700 I won that made the rest of the season possible. I'll always remember my first real payday, more even than the dinner we had with Prince Albert of Monaco in Evian, the French home of the spring water. In the third stage of the Iron Tour, I even ran away from five-time world triathlon champion Simon Lessing, sadly only to have my hero refuse to shake my hand at the finish. That first paycheque, combined with besting Lessing, if only for a stage, made me feel like a true professional.

It was during the Canadian Duathlon Championships of 1996 that I found myself breaking away on the bike alongside Peter Reid, a Canadian-legend-in-the-making who would later win three Ironman Hawaii world titles at Kona. After the race, in which we had a sprint finish and I had to throw up at the finish line to beat him, Peter casually strolled up and said, "I'm out in Victoria now. It's the place to be in Canada for outdoor training. Mild winters. Never snows. I hear you're good. You should move out."

I left university to run around France in my Speedo...In 1996 I joined three other Canadians on team Danone and raced the French Iron Tour, eight races in nine days, from Montpellier to Paris. That's me in the hat (back row, centre).

And so I did in November of 1997.

Peter picked me up at the ferry terminal, we stopped off at a mattress store and got the best deal we could haggle. Peter issued his first lesson of many: "Recovery is everything. Train hard, recover hard. You'll need quality sleep. Always buy a good mattress." The mattress ended up on the floor of a rental house near the Crystal Pool that I shared with three other young triathletes, Bruce Davison, Brendan Brazier and Grant Bullington.

After three months figuring out the ins and outs of picturesque and tidy Victoria, braving our first rainy season in the BC capital and learning to live together, we set up a meeting at the Canadian Centre for Sports Development, which, a decade and way too many name changes later, is known as Pacific Institute for Sports Excellence. It is the national training centre established in Victoria as a legacy of the 1994 Commonwealth Games. We told them what the newest Olympic sport of triathlon was about. Roger Skillings, the quietly studious then-CEO of CCSD, was impressed enough that we had ourselves an actual national training centre—basically four guys in their early twenties living in a Victoria rental house. It wasn't exactly Animal House but neither was it Brideshead.

We needed coaching and technical expertise, and Barrie Shepley came out from Toronto to get the centre started, while also attending the National Coaching Institute based in Victoria. Later, Lance Watson came to coach, with Neil Harvey handling the swimming duties, and Paul Regensburg arriving from Fort McMurray, Alberta, to manage the centre. Paul was an expert at repairing bridges and building new ones with local and national sports governing bodies and the like. It was rocky at times, and coaches and administrators would change over the years, but we at least had a structure of some sort to begin something with. We all secretly, and perhaps not so secretly, harboured our hopes and dreams at that time. Yet nobody could predict then the Olympic and Ironman glories to come from this tight little group that started so humbly in Victoria.

We had a great squad training in Victoria before the Sydney Olympics. Led by Lance Watson (middle row, far left), Neil Harvey (front row, far left) and Paul Regensburg (back row, 2nd to left), we started the National Triathlon Centre. It's been through some changes over the years, but the goal remains the same: world-class athletic excellence. Other faces to note: Greg Bennett (middle row, 2nd to left), Brent McMahon (middle row, far right), and me (back row, far left).

COACH LANCE

Lance Watson coached me for nearly ten years and through two Summer Olympics—Sydney 2000 and Athens 2004. He has seen me at both my best and worst, and we shared many racing and life adventures together. He is among the best in the world at what he does. I asked Lance to give his thoughts and philosophy on coaching:

Every person on the start line of a triathlon, whether it is a local sprint event or a World Cup, has a goal that they are looking to achieve. For some it may just be to finish the race and have fun. Others may want to finish feeling strong or in a certain time, and still others will be looking for a top placing. Success starts with a belief—a dream—that you can achieve. This dream gives birth to reality. However, before you can chase your dreams, you must know exactly what they are and where you are in relation to them.

You must also have the courage to make your own rules and not allow yourself to be governed by perceived or imposed limitations. Striving for your dream goal, whether it be winning the gold medal such as Simon did, getting a medical degree, volunteering in Africa or flying the space shuttle, should be the fuel that gives your days meaning and purpose. No one can tell you what is important in your life. That is your decision and should be something that pulls fiercely at your heart and your soul.

It is clear that successful athletes like Simon are highly committed to excellence. There is no way to achieve a high level of excellence in your training without a high level of commitment. The key to being successful is to commit to excellence in your pursuit of your dream. Don't cut corners, and be passionate about the journey.

Establishing what your dream goal is becomes the first step. The next step is to develop a strategy as to how you strive for that goal.

Firstly, write down your goals. Write out your long-term "dream goal" and your step-by-step process to achieve this goal. Make sure the steps are logical and one set leads to the next. Athletes create times of the year to work on certain skills, times to focus on building fitness and times to rehearse race tactics and strategies. Those are all steps to achieving their goals. If you are not sure, then research or consult someone who has already achieved what you want to achieve. How did they do it? Where did they go to learn? Work on your step-by-step goals weekly and daily. Make sure you refer back to these written words to maintain your focus and commitment.

Secondly, you should share your goals. Don't be afraid to tell the people close to you what you want to achieve. A social-support system can help you stay on track when times get tough. Often when athletes are struggling with their training or racing, a coach, friend or parent can help them remain calm and maintain their training commitment.

Finally, visualize your goals. See yourself achieving everything you have written down. Simon visualized every detail of his racing performance. All the small technical details, such as start position in the water, proper transitions, pedal cadence on the bike and relaxed arms while running, helped propel him to achieving his dream goal. These details will help translate visualization into reality. This imagery engages your thoughts, emotions and feelings, and more importantly, it fosters self-belief.

Simon's Scrapbook: Sydney 2000

Me and Coach Lance

Very proud to bear the flag at the Closing Ceremonies

Extreme closeup of Steve Nash

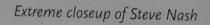

Amazing man, amazing competitor. Hamish Carter and some crazy Canuck.

A big hug for Dad

Kate and Jess, number-one fans

The lucky cake worked!

Who's that guy on the cereal box? Oh wait, that's me...

CHAPTER 6

Manchester

The Summer Olympics quadrennial between Sydney 2000 and Athens 2004 was a strange one, filled with highs and lows. Getting off the plane at Victoria airport following Sydney, Olympic gold medal around my neck, was a rare experience. The terminal was jammed, and chants of "Simon, Simon, Simon..." boomed out and filled the air. This was repeated at the many school assemblies I was invited to after my return. "Simon, Simon, Simon..." was always ear-splitting. Was this really all for me? Was this really my life? What it did prove was what an inspiration the Olympics are to young people. I was quoted in the *Victoria Times Colonist* at the time, and I still hope my success, and that of any athlete, has this effect: "It hopefully creates in children a love of fitness that they can carry with them into their lives."

This was the outside Simon. Inside, I was a very competitive little bugger. In soccer, I loved winning. But it was even better when I scored all the goals. I was always that under-sized and sometimes dismissed little guy with the competitive streak who would show them. And I did—on the greatest sporting stage of all! I showed them.

I think my mom is staring at the camera and thinking exactly what I'm trying not to think about—How many people are watching this?—as we joined Brian Williams on CBC Sports shortly after my race in Sydney.

But who "them" was I really couldn't quite grasp. I just knew I had done it—gone in to Sydney an unknown and emerged an Olympic champion. The famous picture that kept running through my mind—and which probably best reflected my attitude at the time—was the one of Muhammad Ali glaring and standing over a prone Sonny Liston. See world? See what I can do? That pose wasn't really me, yet I still had this need to prove things to people.

At some point, not too long after I returned from Sydney—and amid all the celebrations and adulation I was receiving—came the panic and paranoia of a single thought: What if I was only a one-hit wonder? That thought, that attitude, carried with me all the way to Athens. My goal was to go to Athens and declare, "Who's a one-hit wonder now, world?"

Clearly, I hadn't yet learned some important lessons about sport and life. This was not always going to be a happy quadrennial. Looking back, I chuckle and know why when growing up there were times when nobody wanted to play soccer with me. Who wants to play with the kid who scores all the goals and revels in it?

Kingston, Ontario, was an amazing place to grow up. People came out to celebrate two Olympians when we came home from Sydney. As a kid I never imagined I'd be at City Hall receiving the "keys to the city."

The 2001 World Championships were set for Canada, in the Alberta capital of Edmonton, and of course I was now very much the centre of attention, coming in as the defending Olympic champion and a bit of a Canadian folk hero. I certainly felt the pressure of racing in the Worlds at home. The crowds came out and the support was fantastic. But in the end it simply wasn't to be my day and I faded to finish in sixth place. I was raging mad that I couldn't pull this off. As Olympic champion, racing at home, nobody was willing to help me along the course in terms of pacing or pack racing. These are ways racers help each other along the course in order to really help themselves. But the rest of the field's attitude to me was "Sorry, Simon. No way." Being Olympic champion will do that to you. I wanted so much to win the World Championships on home soil, but try as I might, that day belonged to Australia's Peter Robertson. The consolation was seeing the 15,000 people at the finish line and knowing our sport had arrived in my home country.

The next year, 2002, was one of ups and downs—one huge high amid a lot of misfortune and disappointment. After the Olympic win, one might think the Commonwealth Games would be a swim, bike ride and run on Easy Street. Right? Far from it, in fact. It's the very nature of "regional" or "special-interest" Games, such as the Commonwealth Games, Pan American Games or Asian Games, that some events are world-class and others aren't. Since so many international triathlon stars hail from Commonwealth nations—me, Peter Robertson, Simon Lessing, Hamish Carter to name just a few—our sport was set to provide a truly memorable set piece at the 2002 Commonwealth Games in Manchester, England, with six former world champions set to compete. And, of course, one Olympic champion.

What I wasn't figuring on was fracturing my collarbone and breaking two bones in each wrist in a nasty fall from the bike during a race at Geelong, Australia, in April of 2002. These injuries were incredibly painful, and the ugly road rash was far from the worst of it. Both arms were in slings, and I would have to be wrapped like a mummy for six weeks. The pundits immediately wrote me off for much of that racing season. Just try going to the toilet with your arms and hands bound tight! It was not an experience I would like to go through again. I was, however, incredibly determined to win at Manchester 2002 and began my comeback training long before anybody else thought practicable. Despite my upper body and arms wrapped in bandages, I walked up and down stairs and around the block for hours at a time in an attempt to keep fit. It worked. The bandages came off, the collarbone and wrists healed and I was, well, at least semifit.

By the time the Manchester 2002 Commonwealth Games rolled around in July, my body felt ready to respond to the challenge of the Games race. Nothing, however, could prepare the team for the tidal wave of emotions that would totally gobsmack us before the race in Manchester. Kelly Guest was a friend and training partner. He worked hard and, against all odds at the trials, made the Canadian team to the Manchester Games in a long-shot upset. It was such a feel-good story and the culmination of a lifetime dream for Kelly. He was, justifiably, over the moon with delight. How all that turned into one of the most brutally depressing and wrenching moments of my racing career—not to mention Kelly's—is still sad to think about. I was stunned when I first heard the news of Kelly's positive drug test, thinking it had to be a mistake. Regretfully it wasn't. The ensuing press conference, which I attended to support Kelly, was one of the most wrenching things I have experienced. Kelly was devastated. So were the rest of us in the Canadian camp.

Kelly Guest, an athlete few outside Canadian triathlon circles had heard of, was suddenly headline news across the nation and the Commonwealth. Kelly's tests showed traces of a banned substance, just over the allowable limit, which was immediately blamed on contaminated supplements. We all knew Kelly hadn't cheated, and an arbitrator later found he had not intentionally done anything to cheat. The mystery of why Kelly tested positive deepened when his supplements were tested by the Canadian Centre for Ethics in Sport (CCES) and they were all clean. Now no one knew why he had tested positive. Sadly, no one seemed to care. They had a positive test. Too bad, so sad, said the powers that be. The Canadian team, following the Canadian Policy on Doping in Sport (2000), reluctantly sent Kelly home, and he sat out a suspension of two years, which effectively sidelined his career. Many triathletes, me included, took the same nutritional supplements as Kelly.

Each athlete must be responsible for what goes into his or her body, said the authorities. And that was that. Later, when we learned that none of Kelly's supplements were contaminated, the official line remained unchanged. There was no curiosity about how Kelly could have tested positive with clean supplements; there was just a slavish adherence to the rules. But, as he later discovered, Kelly has a rare condition known as "active urine," a chemical process that occurs in the urine sample and has nothing to do with ingesting prohibited substances. The recorded levels in his body were so tiny—barely over the limit—that they were likely naturally produced.

We were devastated as we watched Kelly Guest's press conference during the Commonwealth Games. The circumstances took him out of the Games, and I remember thinking how incredibly unfair it was. After that press conference, I went out for a run alone and thought, I'm going to crush this race. (Joel Filliol, Natasha Filliol, Sharon Donnelly, and Simon, L-R)

Needless to say, all of this made for a difficult Games in Manchester. I was to the point of being almost completely distracted from the task at hand. I missed having Kelly beside me at the start line. Our whole Canadian team was not in the best frame of mind.

Through his deep emotional pain, Kelly retained his sense of humour. He e-mailed me shortly after arriving back in Canada, saying he hoped to meet some new girls because of his sudden fame. A dose of humour can go a long way. It was good to laugh again through our tears.

The final chapter in Kelly's tragedy came many years later when the CCES told him they now think his positive test may have been a mistake.

"It was a raw deal that seems even more raw now," Kelly told the *Victoria Times Colonist* in 2009.

But true to Kelly's fighting and forgiving spirit, he has not let bitterness eat away at him. He has continued contributing to the sport, and he coaches the next generation of young triathletes in his Kelly's Kids Triathlon Club.

"Despite all that has happened, this sport has brought the best things in life to me," he told the *Times Colonist*.

That just shows the kind of guy he continues to be. Kelly's attitude has provided me and others a valuable lesson on perspective and perseverance.

I raced at Manchester with Kelly's nickname "Kel Kel" written on the frame of my bike. I raced for myself and for Kelly. I raced with a sense of purpose. Hours before, Carol Montgomery had won the women's triathlon gold for Canada at the age of thirty-five and with an injured foot that had been frozen to let her compete. Carol had had a bad race at the Olympics in Sydney two years earlier, and it was great to see her on top of the podium in Manchester. That was a measure of redemption and a most welcome breakthrough for our women's team, especially after all that had come before at these Commonwealth Games for the Canadian triathletes.

More than 100,000 spectators lined the course as triathlon made its Commonwealth Games debut. I was on a mission in the men's race. Even as my hamstring began to tighten, I thought of Kelly. "Come on Kel Kel...come on Kel Kel...," I muttered stubbornly to myself as I tried to fight my way through the pain to keep moving. All I could think about was Kelly, and the accident in April, and how after all that, I wasn't about to let up now just because my hammy was cramping. And I dreamed of that Guinness I had promised myself after the race.

It was a typically drizzly and dank English summer afternoon. But for me the sun shone that day, especially as I overtook former world champion Chris McCormack of Australia and Stuart Hayes of England, the leaders who were ahead by more than a minute coming off the bike. It was an incredibly satisfying feeling to pass them and come over the Millennium Foot Bridge in first place to breast the finish line at Salford Quays and win the gold medal as Miles Stewart of Australia took silver and my great friend Hamish Carter of New Zealand the bronze.

Here is what I told the *Victoria Times Colonist* immediately after the race: "This is so satisfying, especially with the obstacles I've faced this year. It has definitely been a trying experience, but I've also learned

My favourite photo of my dad and me after I won the Commonwealth Games in Manchester, England. I was on fire that day, just burning to prove so many things. My dad told me later that he was worried about me and that I needed to race with joy. It took a few years to hear him.

a lot from the whole injury thing. I've learned a lot about perspective, about appreciating when you're healthy, the things that you do have. I decided that I was a super healer. I really believe in the self-fulfilling prophecy that you are what you think you are."

Then I was asked The Question: the one about this proving that Olympic glory at Sydney wasn't simply a one-off fluke.

"I don't need to validate Sydney," I told the reporters.

But actually, of course, I did. I didn't want to admit that, but it was there in the back of my head: Who's a one-hit wonder now?

"You're collecting them all, mate," the Aussie Chris McCormack said to me after the race.

Yeah, I guess I was. Driven and needing to prove something to myself and the world, yeah, mate, I guess I was winning them all. But this one was different for a lot of reasons. The remarkable comeback from the injury was one. Mostly, however, this gold medal was for Kelly.

MY BETTER HALF

And better in so many ways. World-class athletes need supportive people to stand behind them, beside them and with them. Jennie has been the most incredible partner, and as is so often the cliché, the rock on which I always lean.

I met Jennie in 2002. She was in a local triathlon club in Victoria, just working out for fun and enjoying the social side of racing in the local races while attending university. My interest in Jennie became a standard joke within our high-performance squad. We would arrive at the pool just as the tri club was finishing, and I would joke to some of the boys, "Is that Jennie girl single?" Even though I knew the answer, somebody would quip back, "Long-term boyfriend." I would shrug and get started on whatever training was on the board.

That was until one day I asked, "Is she single yet?" and Trevor replied, "Wait, I think she is." Well, it was suddenly time to organize a barbecue with the tri club! Jennie and I were inseparable right from the beginning. I had always laughed at couples who wanted to get married within six months of meeting. Yet we lived together and travelled to Europe and throughout British Columbia within three months of meeting. I just love how Jennie tells it like it is. She is so honest and thoughtful. If I'm sidetracked, she quietly yet effectively steers me back on course. Until our daughter was born in 2007, Jennie was the funniest person I knew and now ranks a close second to her hysterical sidekick and little monkey, Pippa.

Jennie is the most caring and wonderful mother, who must now keep an eye on two hooligans. Jennie is the planner and I'm the dreamer. I think outside the box, make crazy plans and move from one thing to the next with an attention span that drives my friends crazy. Yet Jennie quietly, and at times forcefully, steers our lives with balance and intention. That's not to mention the many great laughs she provides. Laughter is important. So is a great life partner. I am fortunate to have both.

CHAPTER 7
Athens 2004

The high of gold at the Manchester 2002 Commonwealth Games in July was followed by the stunning low of placing forty-ninth at the 2002 World Championships in October in Cancun, Mexico. My up and down 2002 had ended on a deep downer. First there was the crash in April at the World Cup race at Geelong, Australia, during which I broke my collarbone and both wrists. I've erased from memory the very difficult trips to the washroom and painful process of such simple things as putting on a T-shirt with both arms in slings. Through grit and drive I was able to recover in time to win the Commonwealth Games, which was hailed in the media as an extraordinary comeback.

I wonder if all the turmoil of that year finally piled up on my shoulders and weighed me down at the Worlds in Cancun. I was exhausted after Manchester and took a three-week break from training to explore British Columbia and look for a plot of land to buy, far away from everyone who wasn't my wife Jennie or a close friend. What happened to Kelly Guest seemed to suck all the joy out of Olympic sport. It just seemed so unfair as it was so clearly inadvertent. Kelly got a two-year ban.

He wasn't even making a living from the sport and now the legal bills were piling up. I needed space from all the pressure and found it on a trip through the Rockies.

By the time World Championships rolled around in October 2002, I just wasn't ready. We had conveniently decided our squad didn't need an acclimatization camp prior to racing in Cancun. The truth was Coach Lance Watson and I were simply tired of travelling. I got to the race unprepared and lacking the passion it takes to perform. Defending world champion Peter Robertson of Australia and Andrew Johns of England, both of whom I beat at the Commonwealth Games, took the silver and bronze medals at the worlds behind winner Ivan Rana of Spain. My great friend Greg Bennett of Australia was fourth. It was happy times in sunny Cancun for everybody except me. So began the toughest two-year stretch of my pro racing career and one that would test and challenge me in ways I never thought possible.

The Olympic gold medal from Sydney, which had carried me to household-name status in the triathlon world, began to weigh me down like an anchor. Now I was that guy with the target on his back. You don't hear whispers of "One-Hit Wonder" without being affected by them. Not if you're somebody as driven as I am. I still had things to prove to people. But there is no joy in that attitude. At this point, I was no longer competing for the pure joy and thrill of the sport. It became clinical and methodical. I was beginning to feel the

TRIATHLON 101

FAMOUS TRIATHLETES, PART ONE:
Simon Whitfield (hey, that's me!), Canada, inaugural Olympic champion at Sydney 2000; Jan Frodeno, Germany, Beijing 2008 Olympic champion; Hamish Carter, New Zealand, Athens 2004 Olympic champion; Simon Lessing, Great Britain, five-time World short-course champion; Emma Snowsill, Australia, Beijing 2008 Olympic women's champion; Brigitte McMahon, Switzerland, inaugural Olympic women's champion at Sydney 2000.

pressure of being the defending Olympic champion. It distracted me from the joy of competing and the opportunities I had before me.

It hung over everything I did. In the Manchester Commonwealth Games, I raced and won with the motto taken from a Snoop Dogg song: "If ya'll don't like me, #@%@#%."

I had a poster on my bedroom wall with Muhammad Ali standing over Sonny Liston, fist clenched by his chest, with the caption written on it: *When you're this good, it's hard to be humble.* When I crossed the finish line in Manchester, I stopped, held my fist to my chest and posed like Ali. I felt I had something to prove. Yet that night, after carrying the Canadian flag into the Closing Ceremonies, I didn't celebrate. I ducked out a side gate while the party was just getting started. I went back and sat in my room at the Athletes Village and stared blankly at the wall.

I might have won in Edmonton, 2003, but something was missing. It wasn't until after the disappointment of Athens a year later that I would regain my perspective.

Coach Lance and I had made it to the top, but we were having trouble staying there. I won some big races in 2003 and the first two World Cup events of 2004. Yet already the rigging on our ship was starting to get tangled and knots were appearing in the lines. We were out front, but the fog was getting thicker and we couldn't admit the rocky shore was coming.

At the Athens 2004 Summer Olympics, we wrecked ourselves on the rocks with full force. We simply didn't know how to handle being the defending Olympic champion. There is no way to hide it or any other way to state it. We did everything wrong. We left our West Coast base in Victoria to train in the BC Interior city of Penticton because its arid surroundings better replicated the conditions we would face in Athens. Penticton is a great sports city—the home of Ironman Canada—but we were away from home base and it's not something we had ever done before. We got away from our core principles. We over-analyzed everything. And we were slightly arrogant—thinking we knew it all. We insulated ourselves from everyone.

The worst moment, and it was nearly a complete meltdown, came during an ill-advised pre-Athens training camp we set up for Brampton, Ontario, less than three weeks before the 2004 Summer Games. The pool was way too hot. I got violently ill from food poisoning and spent an entire night vomiting. Changing venues to Sheridan College didn't help. Because of an allergic reaction to milk, I broke out in hives and was convinced my throat was closing. I began hyperventilating. The trouble was I was driving down the Don Valley Parkway at the time. I careened into a random parking lot and stopped the car. Bystanders thought I was overdosing and called an ambulance. When it arrived, the paramedic immediately saw there was no real physical distress but the signs of an emotional breakdown. He grabbed me and said, "Son, you're okay. Calm down. Get your act together. You're fine. I recognize you. I watched you in Sydney. I know you can win."

I never got his name, but that paramedic was a wonder and I will never forget that. After a trip to the hospital for a quick check, I was released. When I arrived back at the parking lot, I found the inside of the windshield of my rental car caked in a milky slime. In frustration, I had thrown my cappuccino at the windshield. Cleaning it was a sticky mess. But it was nothing like the sticky emotional mess I found myself in at this critical time so close to the Athens Olympics. Being the defending Games champion was definitely getting to me. I went back to Victoria just before the Games to regroup and be with Jennie. I needed a break. I have never before told anyone outside my closest

Jennie and me in Athens. I feel incredibly lucky and blessed to be with Jennie; we're two kids navigating our way together. I remember thinking, Whatever happens tomorrow, let's just get in a car and get lost in Europe. *Her only thought was,* I'm driving.

circle about this near emotional collapse. But there was no time to analyze it. Athens was upon us.

The Canadian triathlon team arrived in Athens in three waves: Lance and myself by ourselves, the staff and then the other athletes. While the others seemed free to race, enjoy the Olympics and perform without any pressure outside of the expectations they had of themselves, I was in a different position altogether. I applaud the efforts made by the others on the 2004 Canadian Olympic team— Brent McMahon, Samantha McGlone, Carol Montgomery and Jill Savege. They weren't distracted by our "prima donna" antics and just remained focused on their own races. Brent had been injured most of the year, yet set about performing the best he could and thoroughly enjoying the Olympic experience. He was a great teammate. If only I could have taken his lead, taken a deep breath and just enjoyed the experience as I had in Sydney. But, of course, I couldn't. I was the defending champion.

A few days before the Olympic race in Athens, the Canadian triathletes were headed to a training session. We were hanging around the van waiting to leave and realized no one had the keys. The tension was palpable and voices began to rise. No one wanted to be held accountable, especially if that meant running back up the five flights of stairs to the condo where the keys lay. I have a vivid memory of that moment—of the tension ready to explode. That's when, all of a sudden, Brent stepped into the middle of everyone and said, "I forgot the keys! High five to me!" He jumped into the air and high-fived himself before bounding up the stairs to save us from an ugly yelling match.

Still, the setbacks and pressure kept mounting. They were both self-inflicted and seemingly fate-induced. I came to Athens just looking for something positive after that frightening episode in Brampton—something to get me to the start line headed in the right direction. Instead, I stumbled headlong into my first obstacle—the food. No one had planned anything in terms of our meals. I arrived at 7:00 PM from Geneva and, after two hours of staging, accreditation and commuting to our accommodation, was simply famished. Eventually we found a hole-in-the-wall pizza joint and ate tomato and cheese pizza for dinner at 10:00 PM—far from an ideal meal only days before my Olympic race.

In Athens the accommodation situation was an unfortunate metaphor for the team's priorities. The coaches lived in a Mediterranean villa overlooking the Olympic course. The Canadian triathletes were housed ten kilometres away in a strange hotel with a kitchen the size of powerboat galley. While we had money to spend on a lavish friends-and-family reception two days before the race, we had made subpar arrangements for food and accommodation. But these details were only the peripheral reasons we were headed for the rocks. While Lance and I tried our best to man the ship, it was apparent that people were already jumping into the lifeboats and heading for safer ground before the race had even started.

We had completely over-thought the preparations for the 2004 Olympics and the tactics for the race itself. We knew to a tee the water temperatures and the road elevations at the sun-drenched Olympic triathlon venue at the seaside community of Vouliagmeni, Greece. We studied everything but learned nothing. We had worked on my top-end swimming speed but had unintentionally paid little attention to my overall swimming strength. That was a mistake that meant

that, while I had the speed to start quickly, I lacked the strength to maintain that pace. I made it to the first turn in a decent position but faded through the rest of the swim and exited at the back of the second pack.

Although I came out of the water poorly, I actually had a chance to recover on the bike and was with Kiwi Hamish Carter and Aussie Greg Bennett leading the chase group up the first hill. I remember that moment in full colour. I sat back halfway up the hill. I hadn't raced much that year, and one thing racing does is keep you sharp and better able to make critical decisions. I sat back, not because the effort was so high but that I felt the pack was going to come together as soon as we crested the hill. I thought Benno, our nickname for Greg Bennett,

It just wasn't meant to happen, and you could see it in my eyes. I simply lost focus in the process and was fixated on the outcome in Athens. I can't believe how much I learned from that experience.

was making a mistake and wasting energy. I was wrong and temporarily stranded alone between two packs. I was not strong enough to bridge up by myself. I watched helplessly as the winning break steam-rolled ahead and I was swallowed up by a chase pack that had neither the will nor skill to organize and chase. That critical decision, that stupid rookie mistake, cost me dearly in Athens. I later tried to tell myself it was a gamble that was right to take. But it proved to be the end of any hope of defending my Olympic title. I failed to recover from that tactical blunder and finished eleventh overall.

From first to eleventh at the Olympic Games in four short years. The only consolation was seeing my friend, Hamish Carter of New Zealand, crossing the line in first place to take the Olympic gold medal many had predicted for him four years previous in Sydney. It was a sweet moment for Hamish, and I was truly happy for him. Another friend and Kiwi, Bevan Docherty, took silver and Sven Riederer of Switzerland the bronze. My big brother, Greg Bennett of Australia, just failed to overtake Riederer for bronze and settled for fourth place.

I practically strolled across the finish line. In essence, I was protesting. As soon as it really started hurting, I gave up. You have a conversation with yourself at certain key junctures of a race. This wasn't a good one.

I was so happy for Hamish Carter. What an incredible athlete, but more importantly, what an absolutely amazing person. I've looked up to Hamish for years, a father of two with a sense of humour and humility unmatched.

I would have that same conversation during the Beijing Olympic race four years later, with a response and result that would turn out vastly different. But this was Athens and four years—in either direction, looking back to Sydney or ahead to Beijing—seemed an eternity.

Athens was the low point. Yet it would turn into an important one, a touchstone from which to learn and rebuild.

I was, rightfully, at the mercy of much post-Games second-guessing by others. I was quickly chopped down from my former perch as defending Olympic champion—and of course the higher you are, the farther you fall. Everyone became an instant expert on our failures. Coach Lance and I were still in shock as others came to sharpen their axes in pursuit of us. The line between friend and foe became blurred. It was like people were quick to praise, keen to ride and faster to chop. Were they helping with one hand while holding the axes behind their backs with the other?

Teammates. Brent McMahon was brilliant at the Olympics. He went in injured, and I'm sure he didn't have the race he wanted, but he had perspective and enjoyed every minute of the Games.

When I arrived back home from Athens, the headline in the *Victoria Times Colonist* newspaper read: "What a Difference Four Years Makes for Whitfield." The rest of the story went on to say, "This time, the arrivals area of Victoria International Airport wasn't packed with adoring kids. This time, cascading chants of 'Simon, Simon...' didn't reverberate off the walls. This time, there was no Olympic gold medal hanging from the neck."

Indeed, from Olympic hero to Olympic also-ran. What a difference a four-year Olympic cycle makes!

I told the *Times Colonist* at the airport, "The contrast [between arriving from Athens and Sydney] is kind of funny. It's a different reality. When I arrived here from Sydney, I was bleary-eyed from the experience. Tonight, I'm bleary-eyed from the trip."

A different reality, indeed. I was no longer defending Olympic champion. But Athens was the best thing that happened to me. If I had placed third or fourth, then Beijing 2008 would not have happened the way it did. We would have continued with the bad habits and bad choices that were building up. Athens forced us to take a step back and realize we needed to take care of the little details and rediscover the joy of sport that was lacking. But it was a slow process.

The following year, 2005, felt like a detached experience. That year, we were just trying to regroup. I spent the summer with Hamish Carter, the Athens Olympic champion, and that really turned things around for me. Watching Hamish with his young family opened my eyes to living life with the proper priorities: Have fun and enjoy the ride that life has to offer. Take a breath. Jennie and I started talking about our life beyond sport.

ATHLETES, ARTISTS ADMIRED

People often ask which athletes, artists or cultural performers most inspire me and have most influenced my life. In sports, it is Steve Nash. He comes from my adopted hometown of Victoria and rose to twice become the Most Valuable Player of the National Basketball Association. How's that for an unlikely Canadian success story?

Steve seems almost amazingly perfect, with his tremendous charity works mixed with his high skill levels on the court. He hasn't forgotten the world as a whole outside of sports, and I greatly admire that in him. Plus, he's so darned Canadian. He's the ball distributor and the quiet leader who lifts everybody else and makes everyone around him better. He's the quint-essential Canadian athlete, and I think he's amazing on and off the court.

Another athlete I admire on that level is Hamish Carter of New Zealand, who followed up my gold medal in the inaugural Olympic men's triathlon race at Sydney 2000 by taking the next Olympic gold medal at Athens in 2004. I always liked the way Hamish raced and in many ways emulated him when I was younger. But when I saw Hamish as a dad with his young children, I saw him in another light and it gave me a much more meaningful connection to him, especially now that I too am a father.

Peter Reid is the Canadian triathlon great and three-time Ironman Hawaii champion who I got to know, learn from and train with in Victoria. Peter picked me up from the BC Ferry terminal in November of 1997 when I arrived in Victoria, helped me find a place to stay and said, "Let's get you a good mattress because athletes need good mattresses." I later put Peter on a pedestal, quite intentionally, as something to shoot for and used him as a standard of the level I wanted to achieve and the professional manner in which I wanted to act.

My great early triathlon mentor, Greg Bennett, from my days of living in Australia, has also been hugely influential in my life. Greg taught me about dedication and sacrifice. He fathomed early my sometimes hazardous inclination toward misdirection, and he always seemed to be there with just the right push at just the right time and when I needed it the most. Greg, along with my parents, really taught me that you are the sum of the decisions you make. On those early triathlon days in Oz when I didn't feel like getting out of bed for a training run, he made sure to be there bright and early with a ride waiting. After all, what was a young punk kid going to do when the great Greg Bennett was there to pick him up? You couldn't say no.

You had to get up and go.

The Australian triathlete Craig Walton and Canadian Olympic champion kayaker Adam van Koeverden are other athletes who I learned from by closely observing. Craig taught me to act in a professional manner. Adam is another contemporary of mine, an outstanding world-class athlete and equally compelling human being who is concerned about helping kids from underprivileged nations and has been to Africa in that regard through organizations such as Right to Play.

I have also always looked up to and admired two Canadian female athletes. Olympic rowing great Silken Laumann is another of the amazing athletes to come out of the sporting hotbed of Victoria, and Clara Hughes is a rare Summer and Winter Olympian in cycling and speed skating. I truly admire these two women.

The team I most admired was the Stanley Cup-dynasty Edmonton Oilers ice-hockey club of the 1980s. It just happened that their legendary run came when I was still really into playing road hockey with my friends as a kid in Kingston. I would imagine I was Wayne Gretzky, Mark Messier or Jari Kurri as I popped goals. To like the Oilers in Ontario was a bit sacrilegious, but I admired them for one big reason and maybe even then that said something about my competitiveness: I loved the Oilers because they won!

The musical group Tragically Hip was from my high school in Kingston, and it goes without saying everybody from my community was really into them. But from the arts, the person who most inspires my creative side is Canadian musician and songwriter Hawksley Workman. He's been on a thousand runs with me on my iPod. He is so theatrical and eccentric. Perhaps I see myself reflected in that, or at least I see what I would like myself to be reflected in that. He is what I would want to be if I wasn't a triathlete. It was Hawksley's music I listened to in the lead-up to the Olympic race in Beijing before I won the silver medal. When he heard that in an interview I gave, he invited me backstage during a concert he gave in Victoria. We had a terrific conversation that lasted nearly two hours. It was a moment I will never forget. Another was having dinner at Jim Cuddy's house—with my daughter Pippa at the head of the table and Jim, lead singer of iconic Canadian band Blue Rodeo, at the other end. One of the perks of reaching a certain level of fame and renown is that you get to meet some of your heroes.

Simon's Scrapbook: Athens (and after...)

Mom exploring Athens

Dad and I are ready for our close-up!

Start of the women's triathlon event

ATHENS 2004

ATHENS

Me and Jennie with Marnie McBean, the most decorated Canadian summer Olympian of all time

Me, Mom and Kate on the front steps of our new house...

...definitely a fixer-upper!

Getting there... Our new outdoor oven!

Jennie and I visit with my grandparents

CHAPTER 8

Road to Redemption

Jennie and I settled into a comfortable and happy domestic existence, and she kept me grounded and focused as I began to work my way back from the disaster at Athens. Our daughter PK was born during this period, and life felt fulfilled like never before. My improving race results began to reflect that—sixth at the 2005 World Championships; three top-ten finishes in 2006 World Cup races at Cancun, Mazatlan and Corner Brook; fourth place at the 2007 World Championships in Hamburg; and a number two overall world ranking in 2007.

Yet Sydney still hung over everything I did. In 2000, I had run to glory in the shadow of the Opera House. In some ways, it seemed, I had been trying to run out of that shadow ever since. The moment that had come to define me had become both a boon and curse. Ever since winning the inaugural gold medal in the men's triathlon at the 2000 Summer Olympics, I had had to live up to being Simon Whitfield.

It hadn't always been easy. So much more is expected of an Olympic gold medallist. There had been highs and lows in subsequent

Sometimes you have to be a little crazy. Coach Filliol (left) decided to see if we could climb from 7,000 to 10,000 feet in Flagstaff, Arizona, in January. If I recall correctly there were some tears on that day.

years, from gold at the Manchester 2002 Commonwealth Games to eleventh place at the Athens 2004 Summer Olympics. For anybody else, eleventh at the Olympics would be a credible result.

When I looked back to what happened in 2000, it almost seemed as if I was looking back on a person other than myself—as if it was an out-of-body experience. It seemed like a lifetime ago. And for all intents, it was.

But every once in a while, something would spark a memory of Sydney. Early in 2008, I was reading an article about Gary Hall Jr., the American Olympic gold-medallist in swimming, and thinking about how great it was that this guy had an Olympic gold medal. I guess I was distracted and my mind was drifting. Suddenly my brain clicked into gear and I caught myself...Wait a minute, I have one of those lying around the house too.

That moment of glory, however, happened eight years earlier, and we live in a what-have-you-done-for-me-lately? kind of world.

Since 2004, I had been unable to call myself the defending Olympic champion. The world waits for no one. You are always being judged anew each year. And the distant past often doesn't count for that much.

TRIATHLON 101

FAMOUS TRIATHLETES, PART TWO: *Dave "The Man" Scott, United States, six-time Ironman Hawaii champion; Mark "The Grip" Allen, United States, six-time Ironman Hawaii champion; Peter Reid, Canada, three-time Ironman Hawaii champion; Paula Newby-Fraser, Zimbabwe, the Queen of Kona with eight Ironman Hawaii world titles; Natascha Badmann, Switzerland, six-time Ironman Hawaii women's champion; Lori Bowden, Canada, two-time Ironman Hawaii women's champion; Michellie Jones, Australia, Olympic medallist and World Championships multi-medallist; Eduardo Herrera, Guatemala, the first Special Olympian to compete in Ironman Hawaii; Dick and Rick Hoyt, United States; Dick pulled disabled son Rick in a boat, rode with him on a specially-equipped bike and pushed him in a wheelchair to complete Ironman Hawaii; Scott Rigsby, United States, the first double-leg amputee to race Ironman Hawaii.*

That's why it was so refreshing and invigorating to me to have my career rejuvenated in my early thirties. Being a first-time dad was an important part of that. I felt reborn myself. I was again fit and focused, both physically and emotionally—the 2007 results had reflected that. I had finished fourth at the World Championships in Germany, second in the final overall world rankings, and I would go into the Beijing 2008 Summer Olympics as a medal contender. I felt good. Life was good.

Or it should have been.

For the first time in my career, I had taken some hits from the media and teammates on the road to Beijing because some believed I had used my influence to get Colin Jenkins on our three-member Olympic triathlon team to act solely as my domestique—or pacer. Colin is very fast in the swim and cycling portions, but not as fast in the run. The thinking was that if Colin could keep me in touch with the lead group during the first two sections, that would leave me in good stead and my running ability would take it into the home stretch to the finish line.

Coach Joel Filliol (left) and the eclectic Crystal Pool. Joel was a great new coach. We wrote down some goals, formed a squad at my favourite pool in the world and got down to business. He did an amazing job of keeping us moving forward and focused on the process.

Many national teams have started going with the team approach now, and I strongly believe it's something Canada needs to develop if it wants to keep up with a quickly improving world and continue to enjoy podium finishes. This team approach is nothing new and has long been an accepted part of so-called individual racing sports such as cycling.

This is where the sport is heading. By putting Colin in there, I could keep up with the pace he set during the early and middle portions of the race and could punch through so many other competitors and eliminate them from contention. He fills every gap during the bike portion of the race, pulling me along with him. I felt I needed him on the Canadian team for the Beijing 2008 Summer Games. He's not like my Sherpa bag carrier, and he doesn't have any compromising photos of me. This is simply something I felt needed to be done in order for Canada to reach the podium at Beijing. Colin changes the

In three years Javier Gomez tied me for second all-time in World Cup wins. It took me fourteen years. He's an extraordinary athlete and a terrific guy. I think Pippa is thinking, Daddy, I'll step on his foot!

dynamic of the race. He's a real momentum-keeper. You are not going to win going up against this sort of formidable international competition without every little detail taken care of to give yourself an advantage.

I was hurt by some of the reporting on the issue and disappointed in the slant of the coverage. So much of it was uninformed. I don't like cheap shots. I was not some sort of grand puppeteer manipulating the strings from behind a screen. The whole idea that I was the one pulling the strings is ludicrous. Triathlon Canada made the decision to include Colin on the team. The goal was to have a Canadian reach the podium in Beijing, and that strategy of having Colin set the pace gave us the best shot.

Yet the controversy that strategy created was a reminder, again, that an Olympic year brings out the craziness in everybody, including me. I don't enjoy the Olympic year as much as I do the others in-between. Thank goodness Jennie and PK were there to act as my soothing safety valves through all this. Jennie is great at reminding me of the balance of things.

Heading into Beijing, there was much talk and concern about the pollution. However, it was no problem for us because we stayed well outside of downtown Beijing near our venue, the Ming Tombs Reservoir in the Changping District of northern Beijing. I was more concerned for the fans and athletes near the downtown core and the main Olympic Green areas because of the pollution there.

My greatest concern heading into the 2008 Summer Games wasn't the environment of Beijing but of our sport. Not that it was bad. It was good. Triathlon has evolved so much at the top level. While that's tremendous for the sport, it makes it that much tougher to win. I used to be so weak in the swim. I got away with that a few years ago but can't now. The top-end speed is

What can I say? Jennie and I have fun. We laugh a lot. She's simply the funniest person I know.

so much faster in all three disciplines of swimming, cycling and running. The eight years had gone quickly, and it was a matter of keeping up with the increasing pace and the evolution of our sport.

Yes, it's still basically as simple as uttering the cliché that the fittest athlete will win. Yet again, even with superior fitness, the fields have become so strong that if you blunder tactically, it's nearly impossible to make up a deficit to challenge late in the race if you lose touch with the lead group. You must be in that lead group. Hence, the immense value of having brought Colin with us to Beijing. Although Colin wasn't the third-ranked triathlete in Canada, Triathlon Canada named him to the Olympic squad, along with me and Paul Tichelaar, because the national organization knew Colin's value went beyond mere national ranking. That choice would be vindicated.

ON TRAINING

I am, of course, always being asked for training tips. People are surprised when I don't have a magic regimen that is assured to work or how little I really care about the technicalities of muscles mass, heart rates, core training and the like.

It wasn't until after the Athens 2004 Summer Olympics that it hit me. When I looked back at our training, the environment we had built at Saanich Commonwealth Place pool in Victoria, I realized there were just so many people involved. There were sports-science people—and they do valuable work—monitoring my every move, stroke, breath and heartbeat with cameras, underwater mirrors and devices hooked up to my body and then downloaded to laptops. It became a circus and we were distracted. We had paralysis through analysis. Basically, this is about swimming, cycling and running and doing it fast. Let's just do that. There is a lot to be said for sports science, but there's also a lot to be said for simply going out and doing the work the old-fashioned way and "getting 'er done." Or as the captain of my boarding house in Australia used to say, "the hard yards."

After 2004 and a serious shakeup at the National Triathlon Centre in Victoria, that's exactly what we did. We did "the hard yards." We took our little group, moved down to just one lane at the "other" pool in the not so trendy part of Victoria and just swam. We had a broken clock, no white boards, no heart-rate monitors, stroke monitors, cameras or swim specialists. We just dove right into "the hard yards." We cycled and ran without guys from labs with laptop computers monitoring our every heartbeat. We logged the miles, bonded as a squad, and Coach Joel Filliol simply said, "You will rise to the level of expectation." And at Beijing we would. At one point in our training, almost every session was marked by the term "N+1." This meant that the number of intervals to be done wasn't announced beforehand. Coach Joel would gauge the number based on how we looked and we'd try and do one more.

N+1.

This certainly threw off a lot of athletes who were new to the squad. At the start of the session, we would chuckle as they fidgeted and always asked the same question: "Excuse me, how many are we doing?" Joel would reply, "We'll see." That would be followed by a "Does that mean we'll see five or we'll see ten?" Joel's reply, "We'll see." The newbie would then seek council in an athlete who had been there awhile. "What does 'we'll see' mean?" they asked. "It means N+1," the veterans would reply. And the newbies would look back, simply confused. But they soon got it.

The advice I offer parents and youngsters is my philosophy of training, comprising three words: Speed, Speed, Speed.

We tend to overcomplicate our lives in sport when things are really very simple. Go to a park, kick a soccer ball and chase it as fast as you can. Make a game of it. Have fun. Speed comes.

Those involved in individual sports can sometimes get off track just because it is more self-centred than team sports. Many parents ask me things such as, "When should I put my son or daughter in their first 5K race?" or, "Is twelve years old too early to put them in a first marathon?"

First and foremost, I love team sports. Often the individual sports flow out of that. At least they did for me, and my own experiences are all that I can draw from. I played tons of soccer growing up, with ample ice hockey and basketball thrown in. My first individual sport was actually tennis. All those pursuits built up my speed. I just happened to run. It wasn't my main sport or what I set out to do. Because I was fast in my team sports, I went out for track. But it wasn't until I was in grade eleven that I ran seriously as a sporting pursuit in itself. It was playing soccer that taught me the most about movement and coordination. I swam, I rode and I played soccer. I remember one of the prominent high-school running coaches approaching my dad when I was in grade nine and saying, "Geoff, your son really should be just running. He's fast; he should be focused on just running." My dad would have smiled, adjusted his glasses, complete with their taped-up bridge, and said, "Simon loves soccer. He will run and play soccer and play tennis because he loves sports. When it's time to run, it will find him and he will find it."

Specific to high-performance endurance sport, the most important thing learned after my years of competition is that it isn't about he who trains hardest. It's about he who recovers from the most training. Recovery is of prime importance—the ability of your body not to wear down but to bounce back after strenuous training and racing. It's the ability to recover from "the hardest yards." I get injured so little, and I believe that has a lot to do from learning at an early age how to handle physicality in the hurly-burly of body contact that happens in team sports.

THE WORKMAN RULES

No music has inspired me more than that of Hawksley Workman. It is always with me in the running portion of my training, my earphones stuck in my ears. It moves and motivates me. In many ways, Hawksley's journey in music has paralleled mine in sports. We're both just a couple of Canadian guys who followed our dreams and worked hard to achieve them—with a lot of dedication, good people who supported us and not a little bit of luck along the way. I asked Hawksley to relate his story and contribute to this book, and this is what he has to say about dreaming, achieving and finding your life's path:

Although it has been said many times by many people, I like to quote Jay-Z by saying, "This ain't the life that I chose, but the life that chose me." I can look back and see many pivotal moments. But sometimes I laugh to myself, realizing that many of the "big" decisions were somehow made for me. That I am here, via some circuitous path, was largely a blind journey. Guided by intuition? Naïvety? Luck?

I did grow up in a house with a father who played the drums. He also collected records, and music was always on at home—mostly Motown and sixties pure pop. For me, constant music seemed quite normal. We had a drum set in the house, and I started tapping away when I was about four or five years old. By ten years old, I had decided that I was going to seek to become great. I cite Michael Jackson as being a huge influence. The power and excitement of his music and dancing was being felt and celebrated by everyone (it seemed) around 1983, with his album Thriller. We were lucky that great talents still existed in pop music back then.

From age ten to eighteen I practised tirelessly. I lived nothing but music. I played in the morning and put pillows on the drums so I could practise them in the middle of the night. As it happens, the drums were in the family room with the TV, and my parents let me practise during the commercials on the nights when we would all be home watching our favourite shows.

This leads me to the biggest variable of all—people. My parents were incredibly supportive. People at my church were supportive. Many teachers were supportive, and the ones that weren't served as obstacles to simply overcome and gain strength by. I could just as easily have had neighbours calling the police about the constant noise, but instead I had neighbours that relished a little kid so enthralled with what he was doing.

At seventeen, I quit high school and joined a travelling musical and really never looked back. I had learned through all of those years to trust my inner voice. I lived in some pretty dodgy apartments along the way. But I was possessed, and no amount of discomfort would have swayed me.

I believe that the story of anyone who has sacrificed and pursued greatness, whether athletic, musical, academic, in trades, literature or whatever, would be quite the same. I love whatever it is that burns in me. But like any good love, it has moments of despair and ache. I sometimes say I wouldn't wish it on anyone, but I am grateful for the road it has taken me down.

Simon's Scrapbook: Training for Beijing

The crazy things we do to recover after a tough training session

Proud papa! On the way to my first race after Pippa was born

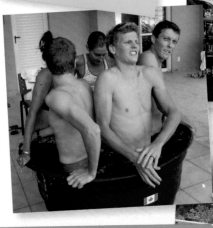

Colin Jenkins and I conquering the Observatory Climb just weeks before Beijing

On the podium in Minneapolis with future Olympic Champion Emma Snowsill

Old friend and absolutely priceless training partner Daniel "Dano" Wells

Colin and I hamming it up

Mr. Work Ethic, Kyle Jones, testing out the ice vests we would use in Beijing

Putting in "the hard yards" on the track

CHAPTER 9
Beijing 2008

Because of the timing of my races, I have never marched in the Olympic Opening Ceremonies, and I kept that record intact when the Beijing Summer Games opened on August 8, 2008. Because the men's triathlon race wasn't until August 19, Coach Joel Filliol and I felt it best to stick to my regular training routine as much as possible until race day. That meant not actually flying into Beijing until after the Opening Ceremonies. Beijing was strictly about the Olympic race, not about sightseeing or taking in the extravaganza beforehand.

I gathered with Jennie, PK, friends and supporters for a casual "Opening Ceremonies" of our own at Fort Street Cycles in Victoria and had a great time watching on TV the festivities across the Pacific as my buddy and Athens Olympic gold-medal kayaker, Adam van Koeverden, proudly carried in the Canadian flag and NBA star Yao Ming the flag for the host nation of China in the magnificent Bird's Nest Stadium. When the final torchbearer, suspended by cables, "ran" around the rim high atop the mighty stadium to light the torch, I had goosebumps because I knew we had done everything we could to prepare.

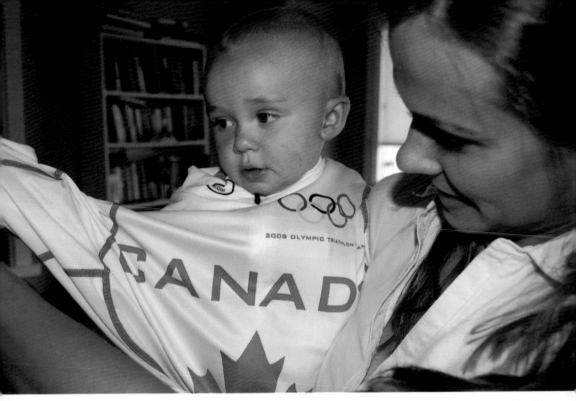

Pippa doesn't know what to think. Decked out in Canada gear on her way to the airport to see Daddy off to the Olympics. I hope to bring her to London 2012, in a shirt that fits.

A great many people volunteered their time and efforts to support the Canadian triathlon team in so many important ways in Beijing. Much was made of the six-racer Canadian Olympic triathlon team renting our own villa and taking what was described as a small army. But the reality was that we had a support staff of five—the massage therapist, chiropractor, doctor, chef and bike mechanic. All of these individuals were trusted not only for their world-class skills but also for the positive attitude they would bring to the circus that the Olympics can be.

The 2008 Summer Olympics triathlon venue was far from the Athletes Village and the central city—in the much quieter Ming Tombs Reservoir area—as we thought it wise in terms of logistics and acclimatization to be as close as possible to the race site. We dubbed the rented villa "McMansion." It was walking distance from the Olympic triathlon venue and became our base of operations in Beijing. Triathlon Canada felt it necessary to do whatever possible in order to accomplish what needed to be done. Physically and in terms of racing, I felt completely prepared. I had a great lead-up year in finishing fourth at the 2007 World Championships in Hamburg and second overall in the 2007 International Triathlon Union world points standings. It would have been crazy not to expend the time, effort and money to do every-thing possible, in terms of set-up and support, to boost our chances in Beijing. The one thought that went through my mind was that this is the Olympic year and you must perform in the Olympic year. I had learned the lessons of Athens and would be better prepared this time.

Perhaps the issue that got the most play in the media was the decision to take our own chef, Cosmo Meens of Mo:Le restaurant in Victoria. Going all this way, and on the brink of another Olympian dream, why would anybody leave food and food preparation to chance? The Canadian team members are regulars at Cosmo's restaurant when training in Victoria and love his organic and unvarnished approach to

Cosmo Meens, the spirit of our team. We were committed to the details, and bringing a chef to the games was part of that commitment. Cosmo is a great chef, but his energy was the key. He brought a smile to everyone's face and put "the force" into our food.

nutritional cooking. Not only that, this motorcycle-riding food magician is one of the coolest dudes I know. While his meals gave us the fuel we needed to race, his incredible attitude added so much to the positive energy we all felt emanating from our "McMansion."

Still, I must admit I was a little cautious when I arrived. I couldn't help but wonder if the negative energy we had in Athens might somehow find its way into our midst in Beijing. The support team was already there, and when I opened the huge double doors to our villa, I took a deep breath. From the moment I stepped into the building I could feel a great energy, and it was on. And it was good. Tom Patrick led a support staff that seemed able to perfectly balance having fun while being completely focused on the task at hand. Surrounded by this wonderful support staff, we all felt as much a group of close friends as a world-class team.

 TRIATHLON 101

OFF-SHOOT SPORTS: *Several sports have evolved or sprouted directly from triathlon and are related. They include Ultraman, for those hardy souls who can handle a combined 320 miles of triathlon racing; XTerra, the off-road triathlon for the truly adventurous, which features swimming, mountain biking and trail running; duathlon, a run-bike-run format for people who don't like to get wet; aquathlon, which has swimming and running but has tossed out the spokes and wheels; aquabike, which includes the swimming and cycling and loses the running; winter triathlon, which takes it to the freezer zone with cross-country skiing and either mountain biking or outdoor speed skating topped off by a frigid run in the cold.*

Colin Jenkins and I were in the perfect place emotionally to race. Kyle Jones was there as the Canadian alternate and did everything he could to help out while studiously taking notes for his Olympic debut in London 2012. Kyle and Colin had gone from the young bucks, who I had tried to help mentor, to two of my closet friends. I admired the way they applied themselves and were wholly committed and driven.

Cervélo, a Canadian company, supplied our men's team with bikes, and no one had better equipment. (Joel, Simon, Colin and Paul, L-R)

We'd had our ups and downs, yet had built a very strong friendship and respect. With so many hard yards done together, I felt whatever success I might have in Beijing would be as much their success, and that is something I hope they are very proud of. I certainly appreciate the sacrifices they made. Kyle was incredibly disappointed to not be on the team. He has an inherent belief in himself. I share that sense of confidence. Beijing 2008 might just have been a little too early for him, but his drive and determination will take him to great heights. Colin Jenkins was the greatest teammate I could hope for. He sacrificed so much to get to the Olympics and performed brilliantly. He did everything he could to get to the start line and help Canada win a medal, and I was extremely proud of his effort. As anyone who followed the Triathlon Canada Beijing Olympics campaign knows, there was some controversy with the team selections and quite a bit made of a perceived ill will between Canadian team member Paul Tichelaar and me. Each story has many different sides, and we each recall how things unfold from our own perspective as seen through our own agenda, bias and insecurities. This situation was no different. The Olympic pressure cooker pushes athletes, coaches and officials to the edge at times; and in this case it dismantled a friendship. But life goes on.

The positive energy and focus in our "McMansion" meant any negative distractions could gain no hold, and we simply moved past them with an eye to performance and achieving our own goals. The Canadian women's team shared this focus and gave it their best. I was proud of each of them as I had seen them all struggle through their individual challenges and emerge on the other side stronger and better for the experiences. That too is what the Olympics can do. Podium result or not, the struggle alone to get to the Games and compete makes you a better person.

When Olympic race day arrived, the atmosphere at the start line was a mix of jovial and good-natured humour mixed with nervous energy and downright fright. Jan Frodeno from Germany, who we thought might not be able handle the pressure, looked loose. In fact, I had never seen him look more relaxed. He had a big smile on his face. It was almost as if he knew he was going to have a good race. As it would turn out, I'd be left wishing he'd been a little tenser— too tense to sprint maybe! Yet rumbling beneath it all, of course, was the quiet tension that goes with being at the start line of an Olympic race.

Coach Joel Filliol and I had worked closely in the lead-up years to the Beijing 2008 Summer Games. We had developed an attitude that stated, We would not get off track and would not get thrown off track when we encountered failure. We had frank and honest discussions about what my weaknesses were, and I was not offended. There is a lot of ego involved in being an Olympic-level athlete and sometimes an athlete needs to hear it like it is. Joel gave me my fill of it. He would let me have my say before telling me why I was right or wrong. "Okay, I'll shut up now and you can go back to coaching," I would tell him. It turned into a good partnership on the road to Beijing.

You can become so immersed in an Olympic race that it's good to look for perspective. This is how Joel recounts his Beijing Olympics race experience as my coach:

"The swim was a more tactical swim with no great separations in the water and a large main pack, out together. Colin Jenkins and Simon were out in fine position, mid pack, and didn't have to chase very long on the bikes to crest the first time up the hill at the front of the bunch. Our team tactics were discussed plenty in the Canadian media and it was no secret to the other teams what our strategy would be. So Colin went to the front during those crucial first few laps and controlled the race by chasing down any gaps and keeping the momentum up as needed. Early on during the bike, we were nervous that a break might get away, as my impressions were that it seemed pretty active at the front as different athletes tested out the pack. Colin did a great job keeping the situation under control, and Simon also stayed near the front to keep an eye on things as needed. We really wanted to make sure Simon got the chance to run with the main favourites out of the second turn. We had options to use if needed, and no doubt that saved some level of energy for Simon. When the break of three got away near the end of the bike ride, that was the perfect group to gain a small gap with, and the boys just monitored for counterattacks at that point. Colin led Simon into the second turn in fine position, and Mission Number One was accomplished.

"Early on in the run the pack was a good size, with the big boys perhaps waiting to start their charge, given the hot morning, and not wanting to risk hitting the pace too early, then blowing out with so much on the line. Up until a late point, we hadn't seen Spaniard and race favourite Javier Gomez's usual charge.

"A question I've been asked frequently is whether I thought Simon was done for when he kept having to close small gaps that would open between him and the front three-to-five racers. The answer, of course, is yes. It was worrying. With the hot conditions and level of competition, you don't usually see athletes claw back after being gapped, even

We're off. I'd worked hard on my swimming pre-Beijing, but Javier Gomez (ESP) had taken it to a new level. The best runner was now also the best swimmer, and I had to respond. When I dove into the Ming Tombs Reservoir, I knew I had already done the "hard yards" to match his swim.

if just by small gaps. But Simon was able to come back each time and keep himself in the hunt. Coming into the final straight, I was in my usual position just before the final water stop. I was screaming as loud as I could for him to give everything to get back with the lead pack. It was loud enough that all the spectators and officials around that area were staring at me.

"Finally, the visor was thrown off, and the long kick started. After Simon sped past where I was standing, I hoofed it over the bridge and down to the finish area so I didn't even get to see a lot of the final action. But you could just feel the energy and emotion of the moment. It was right there. Everything we had worked at for four years was coming down to this opportunity over the next sixty seconds. It took Simon much of the back straight to charge back and make contact. A number of people commented that they thought he went too early. I can only say it seemed the best option at the time. Who knows really what might have been, as we'd seen some awesome kicks from Bevan Docherty of New Zealand in the past. And Frodeno was a bit of an unknown. Simon went to the front down the stretch and only a huge charge by Frodeno in the final fifty metres saw the gold slip away into silver.

"The emotion at the finish was overwhelming. Over the years, I'd imagined what sort of response I might have to achieving such a huge goal, but I wasn't really prepared when it actually happened. There was some irony in Simon being out-kicked by a German this time, after Simon out-kicked Vuckovic in Sydney. But Frodeno was ready for the opportunity and took it with a fantastic race and well-timed finish. He was perhaps a bit of a sleeper, but he did have six World Cup podiums coming into Beijing. Bevan Docherty has been so consistent the last few years and now is a two-time Olympic medallist by taking bronze at Beijing behind Frodeno and Simon. And Javier Gomez finishing fourth speaks to the quality of the Olympic podium on the day. Anyone who wanted to medal needed a number of right things to happen on the day and had to be ready for the opportunities when and if they presented themselves, and if needed, to create those opportunities.

"I could not have been more proud of the performances of Colin and Simon as a team, and of the efforts Simon made on the day to come back each time he was gapped. As a coach, you can only hope that all the training preparation in the months and years leading up to a race like the Olympics can prepare an athlete to be ready for the opportunity when it's there. It was not the result of the Olympic silver medal itself, but the way it was won. Simon raced with courage and heart, and that is what seemed to resonate with so many people across Canada and even the world."

That was Joel's view of the Beijing race. What was mine? Joel admitted he was worried when I fell behind and seemingly off the pace. And so was I. My career has been built on winning sprint finishes and kicking from way back when people least expected it. But even I thought I was done. I was in a world of panic. I thought if I don't do something at that moment, I will run out of chances. Something just snapped in me. I would not be denied. Not on this day. Not in this moment. Not at the Olympic Games. If I didn't dig deep at that key moment and at least make one last crack at it, I would always regret it.

So I reached up to my head and threw my visor to the side of the road in defiance. I wasn't done yet, dammit. And I was going to prove it to myself and the world. I summoned every last bit of will-power I had and ran back up to the lead pack of Bevan Docherty, Javier Gomez and Jan Frodeno. It took me two hundred metres to catch them, and when I finally did, there were about three hundred metres to go to the finish line. Initially, I hesitated because I was simply running on fumes. The thought hit for a moment that I might be able to recharge; but I instantly decided it was just time to go whether I had any gas left or not. I could account for Javier. The Spanish great is the best our sport has ever seen. But he has one crack in his racing

I'm really proud to be part of this gang. The boys in Beijing setting up an epic sprint finish that I'm not sure I'll ever stop reliving.

arsenal—he can't sprint. But Bevan Docherty can. I really felt if I left it to Bevan to dictate, the Kiwi star would kick by me with fifty metres to go.

So I took off. Truthfully, I was just trying to bluff. If they were going to beat me, they would have to call my bluff or simply have more left in the tank than this thirty-three-year-old Canadian. I tried to go wide and get a gap, but Bevan and Jan were able to respond. My goal was to get a quick gap and break their spirit and make them settle for second.

Eight years later, proud to represent Canada once again, and oh-so-close to hearing the national anthem another time.

Jan, however, just had too much left. The big German still had gas in the tank. I seized up and just desperately tried to hold him off as he came striding over the top. When he passed me, I couldn't answer. I had nothing left. But in many ways, coming as it did at my age, when many had written me off after Athens, this silver-medal Olympic moment felt truly golden.

The response in Canada was overwhelming, and I was humbled by all the e-mails that poured in. My medal seemed to strike a chord back home and that was gratifying. As we stood on the podium in Beijing, the Ming Tombs shimmering in the background on a bright day, I couldn't help but think about how life comes full circle in so many ironic ways. Jan Frodeno was a nineteen-year-old swimmer when he watched on TV as I overtook his German countryman Stephan Vuckovic to win gold at the Sydney 2000 Summer Olympics. Frodeno was so moved by Vuckovic's silver-medal performance that that was the actual day he became inspired to join triathlon and ramp up his sporting commitment and training to work toward becoming an Olympian himself. Look at what happened. Jan could not possibly have imagined that eight years later, he would be out-sprinting me down the stretch to win Olympic gold and that the tables between Germany and Canada would be turned so dramatically.

I was initially very disappointed to come so close to becoming a two-time Olympic champion only to miss that honour by the narrowest of margins. As Jan screamed out with joy, I was trying to keep my composure and celebrate the fact I'd given everything I had and won a second Olympic medal. I had a quick but emotional moment with my parents as we huddled together and they told me how proud they were. I said to my dad, "I can't believe I was so bloody close." Dad answered, "Sport is poetic. You ran over the top of a German eight years ago, and today a German got you back."

I took off to celebrate. A few things post-race stand out in my mind. Most important of them is the phone call with Jennie, who had stayed back in Canada to take care of our daughter PK. All the

My parents have been so incredibly supportive my whole life. No goal was too high, and they were always proud no matter how I did, as long as I put my best foot forward.

sacrifices Jennie had made, and the joy she expressed, were so special. We are such a great team. Beyond that, it wasn't the medal ceremony or press conference that stood out. Nor was it watching Jan celebrate or Javier, the great champion who was so disappointed, commiserate. It was sharing those brief but special moments with our Canadian team, the support staff and especially Joel, Kyle and Colin. In each case, for different reasons, it was very special to tell them that this Olympic silver medal was in part theirs and a tribute to all the hard work we had done together to achieve it. Kyle was jumping up and down on the fence, and Colin gave me a crushing hug at the finish line.

At the press conference, Jan thanked his German teammate Daniel Unger, who finished sixth, and Bevan thanked his Kiwi teammate Shane Reed, who had sacrificed his race to control the race for Bevan. I did the same and would have tipped my visor to Triathlon Canada's high-performance committee, who had the courage to make some tough decisions. But, of course, that visor was long gone—picked up from the road as a souvenir by somebody. Triathlon Canada had weathered the criticism, and at times ridicule, to make decisions that were geared to winning medals and not just to being popular. They had the courage to be innovative instead of reactionary as they understood that our funding as an Olympic sport depends on winning medals. The Canadian Olympic Committee has challenged the national federations to strive for athletic excellence, to commit to winning medals. Triathlon Canada's decisions and ability to innovate, with a team-racing

I think Pippa wants to give it away. Can I have Daddy back so we can go to the park? I couldn't have done it without the perspective that parenting brought.

approach, was a reflection of that commitment. And when Bevan Docherty thanked his New Zealand teammate, I smiled. We had the courage to do the same. It wasn't gold as in Sydney. But this Olympic silver shines just as bright for many reasons. We partied into the night during the Closing Ceremonies at the remarkable Bird's Nest. For this apparently not-so-creaky thirty-three-year-old, Beijing turned into a thing of beauty.

FULL CIRCLE

The day of my gold-medal victory at the Sydney 2000 Summer Olympics was a crazy blur.

I remember thinking, Is this fame?

I thought about the race, the adulation, the cheering and how proud I was to see the Maple Leaf flag flying high and hearing the anthem. Everything hit me all at once and I scarcely had time to digest it all.

Fast-forward eight years later. And suddenly what happened to me in Sydney is happening to Olympic-champion Jan Frodeno of Germany at the Beijing 2008 Summer Games after he passed me in the stretch drive to cross the finish line just ahead of me.

It was like an out-of-body experience watching the media surround Jan and the big German being swept away in a sea of cheering well-wishers. Where had I seen this movie before?

So this is what it looked like during my day in Sydney, I thought to myself.

And it hit me how much my life had changed that day eight years earlier in Sydney. Silver is special and my medal from Beijing means a great deal to me. But there is only one winner. Gold means that much. From that day forward you are an OLYMPIC CHAMPION and nobody can take that moment away from you.

I am so amazed I was able to see that, eight years on, from the silver-medallist spot. My golden day in Sydney, and those that followed it, are a whirlwind I can barely remember. Watching the gold-medal winner at Beijing up close, but from the outside looking in, put Sydney in perspective for me.

The days following my Olympic gold in Sydney were a hectic hailstorm of activity for me and people close to me. Gold medals at the Olympic Games often become the gold ticket—an all-access pass to any Olympic event, any party, anything happening in and around the Games with prime seating and pampering.

I saw Jan in the Beijing Olympic Athletes Village several days after his triumph there. I had found a quiet corner to be with my thoughts and e-mail my wife Jennie. I hadn't been there five minutes when, lo and behold, a tired and bleary-eyed Jan Frodeno stumbled upon my quiet oasis. By sheer coincidence, Jan, in his search for some peace and tranquility, somewhat miraculously chose the same small corner of the huge Olympic Village to take a moment and regroup. The Olympic champion asked if he could join me. I said, of course. Jan said he needed to get away from it all. I said, "I hear you, dude. And I understand. I've been there." And we talked.

My own moment of calm following gold at Sydney also came days later and also involved a fellow athlete. I was sitting at the quietest table I could find in the Sydney athletes' dining hall, needing a moment to myself, when Canadian Olympic team basketball captain Steve Nash approached and asked if he could sit. Even though Steve was raised in Victoria, and the British Columbia capital is my adopted home, we had never really crossed paths before this moment.

My first reaction was, "Oh my gosh, you're Steve Nash."

Steve was a National Basketball Association star who was having an outstanding Summer Olympics in leading the Team Canada cagers at

Sydney to a surprising 5–2 record, and he would go on to twice be named NBA Most Valuable Player. But Steve had no airs about him and was such a great, humble and grounded guy. He congratulated me, and we talked for nearly two hours about everything—sports, family, life—amazingly while Steve dribbled a ball for practice from a stationary sitting position the entire time!

I needed that chat.

Thanks to Steve, that was my tranquil moment amid the golden storm in Sydney. I was happy to be able to provide Jan with his calming moment in Beijing. Gold, perspective, conversation and life had come full circle for me.

PARENTS AND PARENTHOOD

It was one summer when I was a young and aspiring triathlete that another racer and I were goofing around in the car on the drive home after a race at Muskoka Lake in Ontario. We hadn't raced well and just sort of went through the motions, actually, and I could tell my dad was irritated. I made a smart-ass remark that he was upset because I didn't win. My dad answered, "Simon, I don't care whether you won or didn't. I just care that you didn't give an effort."

I scoffed. Being young and cocky, thinking I knew everything, I really didn't get the message at the time. But in ensuing years, I often thought back to that and used it as a valuable lesson. The most important thing is not that you win, but that you give a good effort. My parents were both incredibly supportive of everything I did and would always emphasize effort over results.

My dad, Geoff, was a senior research scientist for Dupont, and my mother, Linda, worked in early childhood education. Dad grew up in Australia and was gifted enough to have had his choice of engineering schools around the world to attend, including MIT. He chose the University of Alberta. My parents met when dad came to teach at Queen's University in Kingston, Ontario. I learned different things from each.

From my dad I got my analytical side and from my mom my reactive side. While my dad would think rather deeply about the strategy I employed during my races, my mom was the type of person who climbed to the top of a parked bulldozer along the route during my race at the 1999 Pan American Games in Winnipeg to yell, "Go, Quentin, go!" My middle name, as is my dad's and grandfather's, is St. Quentin. Why she would choose to use my middle name at that moment, or climb to the top of a bulldozer to shout it, was very much like my mother. She was spontaneous in the way my father was studious.

My dad dabbled in a bit of cricket and rugby while growing up in Australia, but he was definitely more on the nerdy side. But both my parents were, and are, fully engaged in my career. As it unfolded, my dad would take apart races and reconstruct them with the true mental skills of an engineer and scientist. He loves the challenge of puzzles and would say to me, "This racing thing is just like a puzzle." He realized it was my puzzle to put together but was always there to guide me along the way and to help me think things through.

I perhaps am more reactive like my mother. She has an uncanny ability to roll with things in any situation, and nothing fazes her. Throw in my dad's analytical bent, and it's just the right mix. When those two elements come together in one person, it can be quite an effective combination.

Both my parents were very involved with our schooling and sports as my sister Kate and I grew up. There was a great deal of interaction with other parents involved in our various activities in Kingston. It was a close group of families with the parents heavily involved in the sports activities of their kids. My parents put in the time with me and Kate as we went about our various sporting activities.

Kate, now an engineer in Ottawa, rowed to the national championship level in high school, and my parents always did a fair job of balancing her needs with the attention I was starting to receive in high school with my running. It was an interesting challenge, and they handled it well. Whatever Kate was immersed in, my parents were as fully engaged as they were with my emerging sports career.

Now lessons learned from my parents are being passed down to my young daughter Pippa Kathryn. My wife Jennie and I have gotten into the habit of praising the effort and not specifically the end result. After toddlers' piano class, it's always, "That was a great effort today, Pippa."

Call it a lesson well-learned from my own parents.

The biggest thing about parenthood is the sense of perspective it gives you. After a bad training day or a bad race, I used to have a hard time dropping it. When you are a young athlete, you are selfish and only find happiness if it goes well in sports. If training and competition goes well, you are happy. If it does not go well, you are unhappy. It is a pretty basic and self-centred life. You'll sleep on a mattress on a friend's floor. The competition and training is all that matters.

All that changes when you have a family. All of a sudden, life gets complicated. It must. Pippa doesn't care how training went. She has needs that have to be dealt with, and now, as she chases the cat around the kitchen table. I can't come home as a parent and be down after a bad day of training. It makes you drop your athletic worries, at least for the evening, and focus on family. Being a parent gives you a whole wider perspective.

Simon's Scrapbook: Beijing

Pippa cheers for Daddy at our Olympic send-off party at Fort Street Cycles

Our "McMansion" in Beijing

Coach Joel with the Olympic rings

A candid moment during team photos

The whole team, support staff and all. One of the rare photos of our super massage therapist Kim Ward (far right) and chiropracter Rob "Elbow Grease" Hasegawa (centre)

One of my favourite photos... I felt like we really played a big part in controlling the race

Colin, Coach Joel and me with the silver medal

Colin and I with our medal at CBC studios moments before our first interview

CHAPTER 10

The Road Ahead

Optimistic by nature, I am really excited about the future. Beijing gave me something to build on, and I look forward to the London 2012 Summer Olympics with great expectation. I've learned all things are possible and hope youngsters everywhere can take at least a measure of inspiration from that. If a skinny, unassuming guy like me can reach for the podium, why not everybody? Why not you? It doesn't matter what your podium goal is—in sports, arts or education. Indeed, why not? Never place limits on your dreams, whether they be in sports or any other endeavours you many wish to pursue. Never pre-set limits on your abilities. You will be surprised what you are capable of if you try. I am sure over the next few years I will hear a chorus tell me I'm too old to again reach the podium at London. I don't plan on listening to them, because I know myself better than anybody else. And you know yourself better than anybody else. Believe in yourself and don't let others sell you short or set your goals for you.

Yet also realize that following a dream requires hard work. I have been driven, even relentless, in my pursuit of excellence. Never be afraid of hard work. It is the prerequisite to achieving your dreams. But never lose a sense of balance. And always have fun. What's the point of pursuing a dream that isn't fun and fulfilling to pursue?

A well-rounded outlook is one of the big keys to success. What my career has also taught me, however, is never to take anything for granted. I've stood atop the world at Sydney and fallen to near bottom in a meltdown before Athens. But I bounced back for Beijing.

We are all the sum of our parts, and we are continually learning. Know that and understand that no victory is everlasting and no defeat is final. Learn from both. Gosh knows, I did. Be resilient. I'm still learning—constantly picking the brains of and soaking up information from other athletes—and I will continue to ask questions because I never assume I know too much.

I've loved the journey and where it has taken me and hope it can be a resource or guide for others to also follow their dreams. It's not always easy, but in the end, you may like where those dreams eventually lead.

An interesting postscript to the Beijing Olympic race happened in June 2009, when I was able to reverse the tables on my great Beijing nemesis Jan Frodeno at the $1-million ITU Elite Cup in Des Moines, Iowa, the richest annual race on the international triathlon circuit.

This time I beat the big man from Germany down the stretch to win the race and the US$200,000 prize that went with it. I was able to hold off a huge stretch rally by third-place Frodeno, second-place Brad Kahlefeldt of Australia and fourth-place Kris Gemmell of New Zealand as they desperately tried to charge up behind me. Sorry, not this time fellas. Not happening.

Everybody was obviously buzzing about the prize money in this race. But, as I later told reporters, for me, the sweetest thing was getting another opportunity to race Frodeno in yet another sprint finish. Who could have guessed that would happen again less than a year after Beijing? Only this time, I won. That meant as much to me as the prize purse.

Getting back to winning and the love of competing. I love the emotion in sport: the joy and the sorrow. And also the drama, the comebacks, the relentless pursuit of excellence and everything you learn about yourself. I was celebrating sport here, everything it's given me and the joy found in the process.

On so many occasions during the winter after Beijing, I would jog in training sessions while rerunning the Beijing sprint finish over and over again in my mind. You try not to let it bother you, but as a hyper-competitive international athlete, sometimes it does. Just a few more steps and that Olympic silver would have been gold. It wasn't to be in Beijing. But, as they say, what goes around comes around, and in Des Moines I beat Jan, and it was for real and not in one of my training-run fantasies. Sure, it came ten months too late to put another Olympic gold medal around my neck, but it was oh-so-sweet nonetheless.

ABOUT THE AUTHORS

SIMON WHITFIELD continues to race triathlon internationally and plans to represent Canada at the London Olympics in 2012. He lives in Victoria, British Columbia, with his wife Jennie and young daughter Pippa.

CLEVE DHEENSAW has been a sportswriter with the *Victoria Times Colonist* for twenty-eight years. He has covered a total of six Olympic and Commonwealth Games. This is his sixth book for Orca Book Publishers.

PHOTO CREDITS

All images used are courtesy of the Whitfield family except the following:

The Canadian Press: p. 2 (The Canadian Press/Tom Hanson); p. 11 (The Canadian Press/Adam Butler); p. 61 (The Canadian Press/Andrew Vaughan); p. 67 (Edmonton Sun/The Canadian Press/Tyler Brownbridge); pgs. 71–73 (COC/The Canadian Press/Andre Forget); p. 99 (The Canadian Press/Robert F. Bukaty); p. 101 (COC/The Canadian Press/Mike Ridewood); p. 102 (The Canadian Press/David Guttenfelder)

Joel Filliol: pgs. 81, 83, 90–91, 96, 110–111

Clarke Rodgers/Sportzfoto: p. 114

Victoria Times Colonist: p. 94 (*Times Colonist*/Adrian Lam); p. 104 (*Times Colonist*/Adrian Lam)

Every attempt has been made to locate and properly credit the copyright holders of the images used in this book. Any errors or omissions are entirely accidental.

INDEX

Page numbers in italics refer to photographs.